D0440782

WRONG NUMBER

A NOVEL

Praise for *Wrong Number*

"A gripping plot that revs its engines on page one, accelerates with each new chapter, and doesn't come to a stop until you close the book at its satisfying conclusion."

—ToriAnn Perkey, editor

"Rachelle Christensen weaves a tale of intrigue, suspense, and romance that is sure to please readers of all genres. Aubree's story captured me from the very first page, and her struggles—both internal and external—kept me cheering for her until the very end."

—Nichole Giles, author of *Mormon Mishaps and Mischief*, and *The Sharp Edge of a Knife*

"Rachelle Christensen is an excellent writer with a flair for combining suspense and sweet, heart-warming romance. *Wrong Number* started out fast-paced, kept me wondering what was coming next, and reached a heart-stopping climax—a gripping page-turner the whole way through. I'd highly recommend it!"

—Cindy Beck, *Cup of Comfort* contributor and co-author of *Mormon Mishaps and Mischief.*

✳ ✳ ✳

Award Winner
LDS Storymakers First Chapter Contest
League of Utah Writers

WRONG NUMBER

NUMBER

A NOVEL

RACHELLE J.
CHRISTENSEN

BONNEVILLE BOOKS
SPRINGVILLE, UTAH

© 2010 Rachelle J. Christensen

All rights reserved.

The views expressed within this work are the sole responsibility of the author and do not necessarily reflect the position of Cedar Fort, Inc., or any other entity.

This is a work of fiction. The characters, names, incidents, places, and dialogue are products of the author's imagination, and are not to be construed as real.

No part of this book may be reproduced in any form whatsoever, whether by graphic, visual, electronic, film, microfilm, tape recording, or any other means, without prior written permission of the publisher, except in the case of brief passages embodied in critical reviews and articles.

ISBN 13: 978-1-59955-364-1

Published by Bonneville Books an imprint of Cedar Fort, Inc., 2373 W. 700 S., Springville, UT 84663
Distributed by Cedar Fort, Inc., www.cedarfort.com

LIBRARY OF CONGRESS CATALOGING-IN-PUBLICATION DATA

Christensen, Rachelle J., 1978-
Wrong number / Rachelle J. Christensen.
   p. cm.
Summary: A woman receives a mysterious phone call that places her life in danger.
ISBN 978-1-59955-364-1
1. Suspense fiction, American. I. Title.

PS3603.H743W76 2010
813'.6—dc22

        2009043775

Cover design by Megan Whittier
Cover design © 2010 by Lyle Mortimer
Edited and typeset by Katherine Carter

Printed in the United States of America

10 9 8 7 6 5 4 3 2 1

Printed on acid-free paper

To Mom and Dad—Thanks for passing along the bookworm gene and for always believing in me. And to Steve—for being the tall, dark, and handsome hero in my real-life story.

✳ ✳ ✳

ONE

✳ ✳ ✳

AUBREE DUG THROUGH A pile of papers on the kitchen counter, searching for her cell phone. She finally noticed the familiar silver gleam under a stack of bills. She grabbed the phone, flipped it open, and groaned. The battery was dead.

"My cell phone died again!" Aubree yelled up the stairs. She heard Devin muttering as he climbed out of bed. Plugging the phone in, she watched the empty battery image flash red and frowned. "I can't wait for it to charge."

Devin poked his head around the corner. "How many times have I told you to pick up one of those car chargers?" He ran his fingers through the matted portion of his curly hair and yawned.

Aubree smiled at his disheveled hair and rolled her eyes. "I know. I know." She tapped her foot. "Can I take your phone today?"

"Sure, honey, no problem. I charged it last night."

"Thanks. I brought the paper in for you." She tapped the front page. "I'll read it tonight after you've marked it up."

Devin whistled at her just as she opened the door. "Love you, babe."

Aubree turned and smiled at her husband. "Love you too." She blew him a kiss and stepped out into the crisp morning air.

She unlocked the door to her car and climbed inside, pulling the seat belt over her bulging belly and taking a deep breath—seven months pregnant and still fighting morning sickness. Whenever she was too rushed in the morning, her stomach churned. With another deep breath, she backed her car out of the driveway.

She glanced out the window, and her blue eyes narrowed at the sun, wishing it would go into hibernation for a while. The freckles sprinkled across her nose and arms had multiplied over the summer. Aubree brushed her strawberry-blonde hair away from her face and smiled when she felt her baby move.

As she drove along the busy highway to her real estate office, she turned on Devin's phone and changed the ring tone to a louder setting. She was just about to dial into her phone's system and forward all her calls to Devin's cell, when it rang. The traffic light at the intersection turned red suddenly, and the ringing phone slipped from her hand as she stepped on the brake. Lifting it back to her ear, she heard a harsh voice.

"Tidmore did the job, and the body is hidden in the manhole on 32nd Street like we talked about. By the time they find him, we'll be in the green. The intruder will clear the way." The words were followed by a gruff cackle. Aubree's heart raced. If Devin was playing some kind of trick on her, it wasn't funny.

"Hey, don't I at least get a congrats? What's up with you? I even kept his uniform for you."

Aubree cleared her throat. She was about to speak when a horn blared behind her. The light had turned green. She pressed the gas pedal and said, "I think you have the wrong number." The other line went silent. She looked down at the phone and saw that the call had ended.

The man's voice echoed in her head: "The body is hidden . . . 32nd Street . . . ." She felt the blood pulsing in her ears, and her hands trembled. Maybe it was a prank call; people were always pulling stupid jokes on each other like that.

Aubree pulled her car to the side of the road. She dialed the number to her house, hoping Devin would answer. After four rings, it went to the answering machine, and she hung up. He might be in the shower, or maybe he had left for work early. She looked at the dashboard clock— 7:30 a.m. Devin never left that early. She dialed her own cell number. It went straight to her answering service. The battery hadn't charged enough yet.

She pulled a mini phone book from under her seat and found the listing for the police department. Hoping she wasn't being paranoid, she dialed the number and willed herself to sound calm.

"San Diego Police Department, how may I help you?" A woman's voice greeted her.

"I just received a strange phone call, and I'm not sure if it was a prank. The man said something about hiding a body, and I'm worried."

"Did you recognize the caller's number?" the dispatcher asked.

"No, he called my cell phone and I—"

"Did it sound like anyone you know?"

Aubree frowned. "No, I think it was a wrong number."

"What's your name?"

"Aubree Stewart."

"And your birth date?"

"I'm twenty-eight, I mean—uh—" Aubree bit the end of her fingernail. "Look, I'm on my way to work right now, and I'm running behind. Maybe it was a prank. I wasn't sure what I should do."

"That's okay, ma'am. We can have an officer check things out."

"If you think it's necessary," Aubree said.

"Ma'am, if you think this is anything more than a prank call, it is necessary."

"Okay. The man said the body was hidden in a manhole on 32nd Street." Aubree closed her eyes and tried to control the shiver moving up her spine.

"I'll contact the officer on duty in that area and have him check it out," the dispatcher said.

"I don't want to be a bother."

"Don't worry. Give me your phone number and work address, and if we have any more questions, a detective will contact you."

Aubree gave the dispatcher her information and hung up the phone. She felt even more nervous than before. What if there really was a dead body? Would she be a suspect? Shaking her head, she gripped the steering wheel. Maybe she was overreacting.

She dialed the number to Devin's office and hung up when his answering machine came on. She didn't want to leave a message and have him worry about her, so she shoved the phone into her purse and pulled her car back into the hectic morning traffic.

An uneasy feeling shadowed her all the way to the office. It probably was a prank call, but the way the man had laughed disturbed her.

Aubree called a couple of her clients and made appointments for showings later in the afternoon. She twirled a pencil between her fingers, re-checking the details of a home for sale. It was difficult to stay on task when the man's gruff voice and horrible laugh kept echoing in her head.

At ten o'clock, she called Devin again but still couldn't reach him. She pushed the papers into a pile on her desk and gazed out the window. When someone knocked on her office door, she jumped.

The secretary, Carla, poked her head in and whispered, "There's a police officer outside, and he says he needs to talk to you."

Aubree's pulse accelerated. "Did he say what it was about?"

"No. Are you okay?"

"I think so." Aubree tried to remember to breathe. She got up slowly and walked out of her office. A husky policeman with graying hair stood with a frown at the front desk.

"I'm Aubree Stewart." She tried to ignore the click and grind of the fax machine as it ran out of paper. She noticed the lines and wrinkles on the officer's face and guessed that he was in his late fifties.

"Mrs. Stewart, I'm Officer Haskins." He offered his hand, and Aubree shook it. Her palms felt like she'd just taken off a pair of winter gloves, or maybe his were just unusually cold.

"I wonder if you could come down to the precinct with me to answer a few questions."

"Why?" Aubree felt the blood draining from her face. She noticed bits of sunlight reflecting from his gold-toned watch from the skylight above.

The officer lowered his voice. "It's about the phone call you received this morning."

"Did they find a body?" Aubree said. Carla gasped.

"I'd rather not say too much until we reach the station. Can you come with me?"

Aubree's heart pounded in her ears. She put a hand to her temple and glanced at the couch in the waiting area, wondering if she could make it there before she fainted. The officer moved toward her in alarm, staring at her protruding stomach.

"You'd better lie down for a minute and take some deep breaths. It's dangerous for the baby if you pass out." He helped her to the couch, and Carla brought her a bottle of water.

"Do you want me to call your husband?" she asked.

Aubree nodded and took a sip of the water. Her neck felt hot and clammy. She took a few deep breaths. "Carla, can you get my purse from my office? I'm going to go with this officer. Cancel my appointments for the day."

The officer knelt beside the couch. "I'm sorry to have frightened you that way." He cleared his throat. "Are you sure you're okay?"

"Yes. I have a weak stomach and, well . . ." Aubree patted her belly and tried not to look as miserable as she felt. Her mind kept clicking through scenarios that would explain why the police officer had come to her office. What if they had found a body, and now they thought she had something to do with it?

Carla handed Aubree her purse and a damp paper towel for her forehead. "I can't reach your husband, but I'll keep trying."

"Thanks. You're a lifesaver."

"Do you need to call your doctor?" Carla helped Aubree to her feet.

"No, no, I'll be fine." She concentrated on breathing as the officer helped her to his patrol car, and she wondered where Devin could be. It was usually easy to reach him at work. Aubree thought of the computer programs her husband helped write and repair, and she smiled. Maybe he was listening to some '80s band on his iPod—working "without interruption." Aubree shook her head and hurried to follow the police officer.

Officer Haskins walked a couple paces in front of her, and she noticed he limped slightly, favoring his right leg. He told Aubree they needed a brief statement from her and tried to reassure her. As she leaned back into the seat, she wondered what kind of trouble she faced.

The drive to the police station only took about fifteen minutes, and Aubree tried to think of something to calm her nerves. It was hard to concentrate on anything besides the police radio, which periodically barked reports amid static. She could hear a lot of commotion going on as they neared the station, and the phrase, "10-85 echo, echo confirmed," was repeated several times. She didn't understand the code, but Officer Haskins kept leaning forward to listen, the fibers of his neck stretching with tension. She wondered if the police chatter had something to do with the call she'd reported earlier.

When the patrol car came to a stop, Aubree undid her seat belt with shaking hands. Officer Haskins helped her out of the car. She followed him inside the precinct and blinked as her eyes adjusted from the bright sunlight outdoors to the fluorescent lights of the waiting area.

"Come this way," Officer Haskins said.

Aubree took a few steps to follow him but stopped abruptly and gasped as she felt a brief pain shoot across her abdomen. She winced and held her stomach.

"Are you okay?" Haskins asked.

Biting her lip, she nodded.

"We're just going to the end of this hall, and then you can sit down."

"I think I'd better use the restroom first." She pointed at the sign for the women's bathroom, and he nodded. Aubree hurried inside and locked the stall. As she dialed Devin's work number on the cell phone and listened to it ring, her lip trembled—he still wasn't answering. She'd never been inside a police station before, and she wished Devin could be there. Pausing in front of the bathroom door, she waited for the rising fear to subside.

She tried to reassure herself of her innocence and the validity of her story. She wasn't guilty of anything and had nothing to hide, but Officer Haskins was treating her like a suspect. What if he didn't believe she'd heard about a dead body because of a wrong number? The truth was all she had to rely on, and she couldn't linger in the bathroom, so she decided to face her fears head on.

Opening the door, she smiled at Haskins and walked with him down the hall. A colorful boondoggle hung from his cell phone case, and Aubree surmised that under his crusty exterior, there was a grandpa on the verge of retirement.

Near the end of the hall, Haskins opened a beat-up metal door. Aubree shrank back before taking a step inside the interrogation room. It didn't look exactly like the movies. The walls were painted light blue, and the furniture looked comfortable yet worn. When she saw another officer sitting at the end of a rickety table, she swallowed several times.

He stood and extended his hand. "I'm Detective Rawlings. I'd like to get some more details on the phone call you received today."

"Do I need a lawyer?" Aubree asked.

Two

* * *

"No, I don't think that'll be necessary." Detective Rawlings motioned for her to sit.

Aubree's nose twitched at the woodsy scent of cologne. Detective Rawlings was much younger than his partner, maybe thirty years old, with a goatee and spiked black hair. She stared at his designer wristwatch and pursed her lips.

"Could you at least tell me what's going on?" She eased into a straight-backed chair.

Haskins sat across the table from her and folded his arms. "Well, why don't you tell us what happened first?"

"Do you mind if we record this?" Detective Rawlings pressed a button on a video camera that was set up on a tripod and pointed it at Aubree.

"I guess not, but are you sure I don't need a lawyer?"

Detective Rawlings looked at the camera and then at Aubree. "These are just some routine questions, but we like to have a record." He sat in a chair upholstered with fake leather that squeaked as he pulled it closer to the table.

"Okay." Aubree set her purse on the floor and crossed her ankles. She looked toward the door and then back at the two officers. "This morning, I was on my way to work, and my cell phone rang. I dropped it when I tried to answer. I picked it up and was about to say hello, but someone was already talking, and they said something about a body being hidden in a manhole on 32nd Street." Aubree looked at Detective Rawlings to see his reaction.

He raised his eyebrows and said, "A body in a manhole. Did it sound like the person was joking around?"

"Well, no. That's why it made me feel so uneasy. I think he had the wrong number." Aubree folded her hands across her stomach to hide her nervousness.

"Did you tell him he had the wrong number?" Officer Haskins asked.

"I tried to, but he hung up before I could tell him."

Detective Rawlings leaned forward. "Do you have your cell phone with you?"

"Yes. It's actually my husband's phone." Aubree reached into her purse and grasped Devin's smooth, black cell phone. Her picture was set as the screen saver. "My battery was dead this morning, so he let me take his."

The detective reached for the phone, but Aubree didn't offer it to him. Rawlings pointed at it. "Can you look up the number of this caller in your calls received section?"

"Sure." Aubree punched some buttons until she found the call she was looking for. She pointed at the screen and handed it to Detective Rawlings. "Here it is. I don't recognize the number."

The detective looked at the number and showed Officer Haskins, who jotted it down in a file labeled with her name in bold caps. "Could this be someone your husband knows? One of his co-workers maybe?"

"I don't think so, and I'm sorry, but I haven't been able to reach Devin to see if he knows anything about it. He must be stuck in a meeting at work." Aubree stared at her name on the file and put her hands on her trembling knees.

"Hmm." Officer Haskins continued writing notes. "Why don't you start at the beginning again and tell me everything this guy said."

Aubree gripped the scuffed armrests on her chair. "He said a name. I think it was Tidmore." With eyes closed, she tried to remember the rough voice. "Yes, he said, 'Tidmore did the job, and the body is hidden in the manhole on 32nd Street.' He said it would be months before they found it." Aubree opened her eyes and tried not to stare at the officer's notes. "I didn't say anything because I was so shocked, and then he said something about, didn't he deserve congratulations because he even kept the uniform."

Haskins sat up in his chair so fast he bumped the table with his elbow. "Uniform? He said something about a uniform?"

Aubree gulped and tried to think if she remembered correctly. "Yes, he definitely said, 'I even kept his uniform for you.' And then he hung up."

"Hang on a second." Haskins gave a slight nod to Detective Rawlings and left the room.

Clasping her hands so tightly that her fingers began to tingle, Aubree asked, "May I please call my husband now?"

Detective Rawlings scrutinized her and then looked at the cell phone. "Is this the number of his office?"

Aubree noticed he had brought up the list of numbers she'd called that morning, including the most recent one from the restroom that said 'My Office' by it. Her cheeks grew warm with a blush, and she nodded.

"I'll have Marnie call this number and let your husband know what's going on."

"Do I have to stay here?" Aubree asked.

"Technically you don't, but it would help us if we could at least ask you a few more questions." He tugged on his goatee and stood up. "I'll see if we can reach your husband." He handed her a notebook and a pen. "I think it might be a good idea for you to write down the conversation you heard today. Try to write it word for word, if you can."

"Okay." She watched him walk out the door and heard the handle click as it locked into place. She looked at the notebook then laid her head on the table and swallowed to clear the lump in her throat. A tear spilled down one cheek. She squeezed her eyes shut and exhaled slowly. She didn't want to cry.

The phone call she had received must have had some kind of valuable information in it. Aubree shuddered when she thought about a dead body being found in a manhole. It couldn't be true, but then why was she sitting in this interrogation room? The police must have uncovered some evidence, and now she was a sort of freak witness to a crime that the crusty-voiced man had committed.

Aubree kept her eyes closed and tried to steer her thoughts away from everything around her. She put her hand on her belly and felt a tiny movement. Pushing on her stomach, she felt a soft kick in response and couldn't help but smile. The tiny life inside her was safe and warm from the worries of the outside world.

She glanced at her watch. It was after eleven—where was Devin? He had been acting strange lately. Last night she'd snuggled closer to him in bed and noticed that his body felt tense.

"What's bothering you?" she had asked.

"Nothing," Devin replied.

"Nothing as in what?" She rubbed his back.

Devin flipped over and pulled her closer to him—as close as he could with her growing belly between them. "I'm just wondering how we're going to make it when the rent goes up next month. I'm not sure we can afford to live on my income alone."

Aubree sighed. "We can do it if we have faith. This little child is important, and I don't want someone else raising him."

"Oh, so it's a 'him' now?"

"Maybe. He's so active. I think it might be a boy." She kissed Devin and put her hand on his cheek. "But don't change the subject. We've been saving for a long time. Our savings will get us through if things get tight."

Devin tensed again and then squeezed her even closer.

"You're right. We'll make do, and maybe I'll get a raise soon."

"I love you, Devin. You're going to be a great father."

"You're already a super mom." He kissed the tip of her nose.

Devin usually fell asleep long before Aubree, but she continued to feel the tension in his body, and she fell asleep wondering why he was so worried.

Aubree glanced at the clock again, listened to footsteps pass by the interrogation room, and tapped her fingers on the table. Things would be tight at first with the new baby, but they had been saving for almost two years. She'd been working at a grueling pace as a Realtor in the San Diego area and had done quite well.

Lately, Devin had been suggesting she could still continue to work with a few clients to earn extra income. She shook her head. If times got tough, she could go back to work later, but for now she wasn't going to leave her baby. She'd have to find a way to ease Devin's doubts.

Wiping her eyes, she sat up and began writing what the man had said. *I might as well help the officers and get this over with,* she thought. She struggled to remember the exact words the man had used; her mind kept replaying his hideous laugh. The reference to the body seemed to be the most important part of the conversation, but there was something else.

She rubbed her forehead and tried to recall what he'd said after he revealed the body's hiding place. The light above her made a buzzing noise and flickered intermittently. Aubree stared at the blank lines on the paper and willed herself to remember.

She scribbled a few words—he had said something about money and an intruder. After what seemed like an hour, Aubree heard the handle on the door turn. She lifted her head to see Officer Haskins and Detective Rawlings. They both looked terrible. Haskins licked his lips and swallowed before entering.

"Mrs. Stewart, how are you holding up? Can we get you anything?" Detective Rawlings asked. She noticed his neck was flushed and wondered what was going on.

"You can call me Aubree. And that depends on how much longer I have to be here. I'm starting to get a little hungry." She tried to keep her voice light, but she had an overwhelming feeling that something was very wrong. Officer Haskins glanced at Detective Rawlings as he sat down across from her.

"Aubree, most people call me Haskins, and I'm sure Detective Rawlings won't mind if you call him Cody." Officer Haskins looked directly at her, but she could only concentrate on his Adam's apple going up and down as he swallowed and cleared his throat. "I'm going to tell you why you're here." He moved closer to her, pulling his teeth across his bottom lip. "None of this is going to be easy to hear, but it's important."

He swallowed again, and she could see his pulse beating in his neck, the vein bulged a little under his skin, attesting to his anxiety. She leaned forward, and her shoe scraped against the grit on the linoleum floor. "Just say what you have to say."

"Can I get you anything?" Cody asked, changing the subject. She studied him, looking for some sign as to why he was stalling. She noticed the long, dark lashes surrounding his hazel eyes and the small dimple next to his faltering smile.

"Are you sure I don't need a lawyer? What about my husband? Could he at least be here with me?" Aubree felt the tension in the room rise another notch.

Haskins' face looked pale against his salt and pepper hair. "The phone call you received this morning was definitely not meant to be heard by you, but we're so grateful you reported it." He splayed his fingers out on the table, and Aubree concentrated on the age spots covering the backs of his hands as he continued. "We checked out the manhole on 32nd Street and—" he paused and looked at her as if to gauge how much he should disclose. Aubree sat up in her chair and rolled her shoulders back, trying to appear unafraid.

Haskins rubbed a hand over his jaw. "We found a body."

Aubree leaned back in her seat and covered her mouth.

"I know this is disturbing, Mrs. Stewart, but we feel you should know," Cody said, and he frowned at Haskins.

"The body has not been identified at this point. We put in a search for all missing persons who wore some type of uniform in the San Diego area." Haskins swallowed again and gripped the edge of the table. "But we think this murder is part of something bigger."

Aubree tensed and shook her head. Why were they telling her this? Were they testing her reaction? She wondered if they still suspected her. Cody reached out and patted her arm.

"Don't worry. You're no longer a suspect in this case. Because of your help, we found a man—someone's family member—in that manhole. I want to explain why we're giving you so much information in a crucial case."

Haskins wiped his forehead with the back of his hand. "We wanted to tell you so you would know what you're up against. Have you heard of the California Bureau of Investigation?"

She shook her head.

"The CBI has its own witness protection program, and we would like to place you under temporary custody for a few days until the threat has diminished," Haskins said.

"What threat?" She felt her heart beat faster as she watched a drop of sweat trickle down the side of Haskins' face. Something was making him extremely uncomfortable, and although part of her wished she could run from the room, another part wished he would just spit it out.

Haskins cleared his throat. "There's no easy way to tell you this. We couldn't reach your husband, so we had some officers run by your house to check if he might be there." He hesitated. Aubree leaned forward in her chair, clenching her jaw.

Haskins rubbed his chin and continued. "Your back door had been forced open. The window was broken. We found your husband inside.

He was taken to the hospital." His brown eyes were brimming with sympathy. "I'm sorry. He didn't make it."

"No!" Aubree cried. She tried to stand, but Cody was immediately by her side, gently pulling her back down into her seat.

Haskins knelt beside her chair. "I'm so sorry. We think your husband's murder is connected to the phone call you received today." He patted her back.

Aubree moaned, "No, no." She wanted to get down on the floor and curl up into a ball. She felt the baby kick again and wrapped her arms around her stomach as if she could protect her child from the news she'd just heard. "Please, no. Not Devin. Are you sure it was him?"

"Yes," Cody answered, and Aubree looked at him. His face was flushed, and he wiped his eyes with the back of his hand. "Mrs. Stewart, our coroner is checking for the time of death, but we believe it was within an hour after you received the phone call. What time does your husband usually leave for work?"

Aubree tried to quiet the sobs that were making her entire body shudder. "Around eight o'clock." She wiped her face across the sleeve of her shirt. "Where was he when they found him?"

Haskins hesitated and looked at Aubree. "At the kitchen table."

She clenched her hands into tight fists. Her body felt like it was going numb. Images of Devin flashed through her mind. "How did he die?"

Haskins lowered his head into his hands, rubbed his forehead, and looked into her eyes. "He was shot."

"How, I mean, where—why couldn't they save him?" Aubree cried.

"Mrs. Stewart, I don't think you—"

"Just tell me. I want to know what happened to my husband."

Haskins' voice was just above a whisper. "He was shot in the back of the head."

Aubree felt her stomach churning again and willed herself not to be sick. She dropped her head into her hands.

"There's something else you need to know." Haskins waited until Aubree looked at him. "Your husband was shot through one of the kitchen windows, and then the door was forced open. It was made to look like a robbery. The murderer took your TV and some other electronic equipment, but we think he also took your cell phone because we didn't find it in your home."

"Are you sure?" Aubree cried. "Why would someone kill Devin?" She shook her head. "This can't be happening. He'd barely woken up before I left for work. I didn't even kiss him good-bye." Her eyes stung with hot tears. "Can I go now? Why do I have to stay here if Devin is dead?" The back of her throat burned and she gasped—the emotions were choking her. She wanted to see Devin, but not dead.

Cody leaned forward. "We think after the phone call today, the perpetrator was able to locate the owner of the cell phone he'd accidentally dialed—your husband. He murdered Devin and stole his phone before anything could be discovered. At least, that's what the perpetrator thought he was doing."

Aubree felt sure she was close to the breaking point. She wasn't certain how much more she could take, and Haskins seemed to know that. He leaned on the edge of the table and glanced at his watch.

"Do you want me to wait to tell you the rest?"

"I need someone to help me, to be here with me." She felt tremors in her body and wondered if she was going into shock.

"I'm afraid that's too dangerous for you." Cody pulled his chair closer to Aubree. "By now, whoever killed your husband has figured out he took the wrong phone."

THREE

✳ ✳ ✳

Aᴜʙʀᴇᴇ ᴄᴏᴜʟᴅɴ'ᴛ ʜᴏʟᴅ ɪᴛ in any longer. A wave of fear and nausea swept over her as Cody's explanation became clear. She saw a wastebasket next to the table and struggled to get near it in time. There wasn't much in her stomach, and after she retched, she could see little black dots in the air. Noises in the background grew dim as she sank to the floor.

The fear was a heavy blackness, and Aubree wondered if she was dreaming when she heard an unfamiliar voice. She struggled as she felt a hand on her arm. "Aubree, stay with me. Keep breathing." Haskins spoke to her, but it sounded like it was from a long way off. Aubree relaxed and let the blackness overtake her.

She woke to find three people hovering around her, asking questions, and she felt something tight constricting her left arm. After a moment, she realized they were EMTs and that she was being loaded on a gurney. She just wanted to sleep, but there were noises all around her, and her body was being jostled. A loud whooshing sound vibrated in her ears. Aubree's eyelids fluttered, and she took a deep breath of pure oxygen from the mask over her nose and mouth.

Fifteen bumpy minutes later they rolled her into a hospital room. When someone touched her face, she tried to open her eyes, but they were weighed down with fear.

"She's coming to. Keep that mask on."

A gentle voice broke through the blackness, and Aubree finally found the strength to open her eyes. She turned toward a woman wearing blue scrubs and a stethoscope.

"Hi, Aubree, I'm Dr. Gina Samuels, and I'm going to be monitoring you and the baby. I'm so sorry, honey. It's too much, all this terrible news." The doctor moved Aubree's matted hair from her forehead and placed a cool cloth there.

Aubree looked around, surprised to see she was now in a different room altogether. "Am I in the hospital?"

Dr. Samuels looked at Cody, who bent over Aubree as he spoke, "No, you're in a private medical facility with the California Bureau of Investigation. You came by ambulance. We thought it would be safer for you here."

Then she remembered why she had become sick and passed out: fear. Cody said the killer would now be after her. Was this really happening?

"Here, drink this, and then put the oxygen mask back on for a few more minutes." Dr. Samuels offered her a paper cup. "You're under a lot of stress, and you're very dehydrated. I'm going to be conducting a non-stress test on the baby to make sure he's doing okay. You weren't out for very long, but you've been through a lot."

"Okay, I'll try to drink some," Aubree mumbled. She moved the oxygen mask and gripped the cup. She surveyed the room while taking small sips.

A picture of a flower garden hung on the white, sterile walls. A lamp cast a soft yellow light on the daisies and snapdragons in the painting. On the other side of the room, a burgundy love seat was positioned in front of a TV. The cabinet beside her was filled with medical supplies. "You don't have to take my blood, do you?" she asked.

"No. I'll attach this monitor, and we'll see the baby's heart rate." Dr. Samuels motioned to a screen as she put a belt around Aubree's middle and then clipped on the sensor that would pick up the baby's heartbeat.

"Good. I hate needles," Aubree said. In the pregnancy classes, they had shown an epidural needle, and Devin had squeezed her hand and whispered, "Don't look, okay?"

Aubree clamped her eyes shut as she remembered that Devin was gone. Tears trickled down the sides of her face. She felt a hand on her shoulder, and Dr. Samuels said, "You don't need to worry about your baby. His heart rate is good. I'm concerned about you, though, so we're going to keep an eye on you."

"Thank you." Aubree took another sip of her drink. The cold liquid felt good on her dry throat.

"We'll get you something to eat soon. You must be starved." Dr. Samuels gave a curt nod to Cody and Haskins as she left the room.

Haskins held up his hands. "She's upset at us for throwing everything at you like we did." He took a tentative step forward. "I'm really sorry. We had to act quickly. We're not sure what kind of danger you may be in."

"But are you sure my husband's murder is connected to the call I received?" Aubree rubbed a hand over her eyes and listened to the hum of medical equipment surrounding her.

Haskins shook his head. "We're not positive, but all signs point to that."

Aubree's eyes widened as she noticed the clock on the wall behind Haskins. It was already 3:30 p.m. "I haven't had anything to eat since breakfast. No wonder I passed out."

"Sorry about that. We spent a lot of time in the interrogation room," Cody said. "I'll see if I can hurry them along with some food." He closed the door quietly behind him.

"Can I call my mom?" Aubree asked Haskins.

"We've actually been trying to reach her already. I'll let you know as soon as we talk to her. We'd like to keep you here a few days for protection." Haskins fiddled with the radio hanging on his police belt. "I'm sure she'll want to come out here from Idaho right away."

"How'd you know where—"

"We've already got a ten-page file on you. Don't worry; it's all good stuff." Haskins gave her a thumbs-up.

"So, am I still a suspect?" A chill ran down her spine when she considered the results of the phone call only hours ago. How could Devin really be gone?

Haskins' pager went off and after glancing at the number, he pressed a button to silence it. "No, you've been cleared. There's no way a woman in your condition could've lifted a 275-pound male into a manhole in an upright sitting position. And you're not suspected as an accomplice because you have an alibi for the time of death."

"Well, thanks for the vote of confidence in my moral character," Aubree said, feeling a little miffed. "When was the time of death?"

"Yesterday at about three in the afternoon. We figure he was shot and then moved to the manhole last night."

"And I met with a client yesterday at 2:15 to show houses and didn't finish until 5:00, but I'm sure you knew that."

Haskins wiped his hand across his forehead. "Like I said, I'm very sorry about everything."

Aubree looked at her stomach. The gauzy peach material of her maternity blouse was wrinkled and dirty. She felt grimy and clammy. Cody opened the door and helped a nurse with some food. Aubree's mouth watered as she looked at the tray placed before her. A bowl of minestrone soup and a whole-wheat roll were sitting beside a large slice of carrot cake. She felt guilty for being so hungry. How could she eat at a time like this?

"Go ahead and eat. That baby needs nutrition no matter what's going on in the world." The nurse added a carton of milk to the tray. "When you're finished, you can take a shower right in there." She motioned to a door on the other side of the room, which Aubree guessed was a bathroom.

She stared at the tray and blinked away the moisture in her eyes.

"She's right, you know," Cody said. "It will help to have something in your stomach."

The soup had a zesty smell, and Aubree made herself take a few bites, trying not to think about the turmoil in her life and focusing on her baby instead. She began to feel a bit more alive as she ate, but the tears were right below the surface no matter how many times she swallowed them away.

"We'll give you some privacy now," Haskins said. "We're going to catch a bite, but I'll keep trying to reach your mother."

"Thank you," Aubree said.

When they left the room, her spoon clattered on the tray, and she leaned back on the bed, letting the tears seep from her eyes. Sunlight fell in narrow strips across her bed, and Aubree looked at the window.

The shade was down, but the light shone through the space on the side. Dust particles fell slowly through the beams, and Aubree watched them. Her mind felt numb. With ragged breaths, she tried to keep her thoughts from returning to the moment that morning before she left for work. She couldn't help it. Devin's face flashed through her mind again— his wink, curly brown hair, and easy smile.

She didn't want to think about how it was her fault he was dead. Some rational part of her mind knew it wasn't really—she couldn't control the man who had dialed the wrong number.

Aubree stumbled into the bathroom and turned on the water. She watched the steam rise to the ceiling. Then she stepped inside and let the warm water run over her body. She cried again, trying not to sob too loudly. She wanted a few minutes alone, but what she really needed was her mom. With her head in her hands, she pictured her mom's clear blue eyes—the ones she had inherited.

"Mom, I need you right now," Aubree whispered between ragged breaths. As the water poured over her shoulders, she prayed fervently. "Lord, please help me. I don't know what to do." She tried to ignore the raw pain that bubbled up with each sob and instead searched for a memory of peace. The fluttering motions of the baby reminded her of how excited Devin had been to feel the gentle nudges of their baby. She focused on that memory. Then she swallowed hard, stood, and washed the tears from her face.

After the shower, Aubree felt almost human again. She put on a clean hospital gown rather than wear her dirty, tear-stained clothes. Sitting in a soft chair, upholstered with sage green material, she combed her reddish-blonde hair. Even though she didn't want to cry anymore, she couldn't help it.

All of a sudden, she had become a single mother, and she couldn't get used to the idea that her husband had been murdered. She needed to see him, to see his body, to make sure it was all true, but Haskins had told her she would have to wait until tomorrow. They were going to call the case a 'robbery gone bad' until they could discover what the killer had planned.

Before he left the room, Haskins had informed her that they were going to keep the media out of the loop as long as they could. Soon they would contact Devin's family and release a statement to the press.

She rummaged through her purse until she found her checkbook. Photos of her family decorated the checkbook cover. She sighed when she saw the picture of Devin's family. The photo was six years old, but she kept it close anyway because Devin's parents had passed away five years ago in a house fire. Only Devin's sister, Susie, and brother, Gabe, remained of the Stewart family. Aubree felt terrible that she knew about Devin's death but couldn't talk to anyone.

Aubree heard a light knock at the door, and then Dr. Samuels entered carrying another tray of food. "Now these are just some snacks, in case you get hungry later on. The police are going to be back to ask you a few more questions, and I told them you need your rest after that."

"More questions? About what?" Aubree stood and walked toward the tray of goodies. She wrinkled her nose. "Haven't I answered enough questions?"

"That's what I said, but apparently you haven't." Dr. Samuels shook her head, and her short black hair swished back and forth. "I need to check your vitals and monitor the baby's heart rate one more time, and then I'll be on my way."

Aubree leaned back on the hospital bed awkwardly as Dr. Samuels hooked up the monitor. "Thank you for helping me."

"It's been my pleasure. I'm only sorry it couldn't have been under more pleasant circumstances." Her mouth turned down slightly, and she brushed a stray hair away from her dark eyes. "You're looking great, Aubree. Keep up the good work, and you should have a healthy baby soon."

"I hope so." Aubree swallowed hard, and her lip trembled.

"It's okay to cry, but I want you to concentrate on growing your baby. You've lost your husband, and it's not going to be easy without him, but you've got to try to keep your chin up." Dr. Samuels patted Aubree's wrist and smiled.

Aubree felt anger rising in her chest. How could this woman give her advice only hours after her husband's murder? But as she formed a retort, she looked into Dr. Samuels face and saw genuine concern there. Aubree blinked, and the tears cascaded down her cheeks. She felt Dr. Samuels' arms around her as she cried. After a few minutes, Aubree took a ragged breath and wiped away her tears. "I'll be okay now," she said.

"I have to run along, but I want you to remember what I said. Keep your chin up, keep your mind alert, and be aware of your surroundings."

"Okay." She watched as Dr. Samuels left the room. Why did she sense the doctor knew more than she was saying, as if she were trying to warn her about something?

Aubree thought about Devin and how she'd blown him a kiss that morning. She recalled his sleepy face when he poked his head around the corner to tell her she could borrow his cell phone. She covered her mouth and shook her head.

When he died, Devin was probably doing the same thing he had done every morning since he'd found out she was expecting: reading the morning paper and circling names. Aubree watched the tears fall onto the blue and white hospital gown. He was probably eating a bowl of his favorite bran flakes along with half a banana. He would linger over the paper and run his fingers through his curly brown hair as he read the sports section and circle names with his red pen. Names he liked that he would later talk to Aubree about. Names he wanted to give their child.

Some of them would make Aubree laugh. Devin had been known to circle the names of stores like Kinko's or Panda Express or especially nicknames of athletes. But several things he circled were names he truly liked, and a few times he had marked them with big red stars.

Since their baby had been too shy when Aubree had her ultrasound, the doctor hadn't been able to tell if they were having a boy or a girl. So Devin always circled both boy and girl names, or sometimes he would circle a name like "George" and then write "if it's a girl" beside it. There was a stack of newspapers at home that Aubree had saved with names she especially liked.

She let the images of the newspapers run through her mind and then sobbed even harder. Devin would never know his child. Her husband would never get to hold their baby and say its name. Suddenly, Aubree knew what she had to do.

A few minutes later, another knock announced the entrance of Haskins and Cody.

"I'm sorry to keep bothering you. We have a few more questions," Haskins said as he sat in the chair by her bed.

Aubree sat up and spoke a little louder than she'd intended, "I need to have the paper Devin was reading this morning. Please make sure the police don't ruin it."

Haskins looked puzzled, and Cody frowned. "The paper could be ruined already, and it may be catalogued as evidence."

"I need to see it. It was the last thing my husband read before he died. Please."

"I'll have to check with the investigating officer and see what we can do," Haskins said.

Aubree noticed Cody was holding the notebook she had written in earlier. He coughed and looked at her writing. "I wanted to check with you to see if there's anything else you can remember about the wrong number today."

She shook her head. "I'm sorry. I tried to remember everything he said, but I don't know."

"You've done well to remember what you did," Cody said. "How positive are you about the use of the word *intruder?*"

She raised her eyebrows. "Intruder? He must've said it. I don't know why else it would come to mind."

Haskins turned down some chatter on his radio and looked at Cody. "It seems to stand out, and so we wanted to ask if you could remember exactly how the speaker used the word."

"I'm trying to remember." She picked at a string on the hospital blanket, wishing her brain didn't feel like it was in some kind of fog. She didn't want to hear that voice again—the one they thought was responsible for Devin's murder—but maybe if she could remember what he had said, then she could forget.

"Do you think he said, 'An intruder'? Or, 'The intruder'?" Haskins asked. "I know it's a small thing, but we're working on some leads."

"I'll keep trying to remember. I want to help you find these people." Aubree gripped the blanket in her hand.

"Thank you for trying," Cody said. "Maybe some rest will help."

As soon as the officers left, Aubree yawned. She eased into the bed and pulled the blankets up to her chin. She wanted to escape into the unconscious realm of sleep, and exhaustion was about to overcome her when a thought came to mind. If the killer knew they had the wrong cell phone, he must realize the mistake he'd made in killing Devin.

She'd already reported the information she'd heard to the police—the location of the body—and it had been found. It would probably only be a matter of time before the police tracked down Tidmore. What danger was left to her after he was behind bars? Was she truly in any real danger for the fragment of conversation she'd heard that morning? She doubted it.

Aubree hoped that the police would come to the same conclusion by tomorrow.

FOUR

* * *

THE NEXT MORNING, SUNLIGHT peeked through the blinds and warmed Aubree's face. Opening her swollen eyes, she tried to remember why she was in a hospital bed. Then the realization hit her full force, and she groaned. A clean, citrus smell hung in the air, and she could hear people talking outside her door. Her husband was dead. How could it be true that Devin was gone?

Closing her eyes, she imagined Devin's face and tried to hear his voice, his laughter, anything that would make him feel closer. The edges of her mental picture were fuzzy, and her grief seemed to crowd out happy memories.

Aubree remembered what the doctor had said about taking care of herself. She stretched and sat up slowly, wondering if a walk around the facility would help clear her mind. Before she could get herself out of bed, someone knocked on the door, and Aubree croaked, "Come in."

Haskins pushed opened the door and entered, followed by Cody and another man. Aubree narrowed her eyes, frustrated at the early intrusion.

"I'm so sorry to disturb you this early, but we've got some important information for you." Haskins clenched a folder and a notebook. "We also need to ask a few more questions."

"No. No questions until I can at least go to the bathroom," Aubree snapped. Haskins flinched when she spoke. She pulled her legs over the side of the bed and frowned.

"We'll be back in ten minutes, and we'll bring you some breakfast." Cody stood and motioned for the others to follow.

"Okay." Aubree walked stiffly across the room and slammed the bathroom door. She sank onto the tiled floor and tried to swallow the rising flood of tears.

"Why? Why did this have to happen to me now?" She spoke to the ceiling.

She shook her head, swallowed, and forced herself to clean up. The cool water on her face felt good. She looked at her haggard appearance in the mirror—the stringy hair and dark circles under her eyes. She offered a silent prayer: *Please help me get through this day.* It was all she could ask. If she could get through one day, maybe she'd be able to get through the next.

Aubree wiped her eyes and reentered her room, surprised that the three men hadn't returned yet. She pulled a white hospital blanket from the bed and sat on the green upholstered chair. The air conditioning in the room was on high, and crying had given her the chills. She thought again of her mother and decided to insist that she be allowed to speak to her.

Cody returned first with a steaming plate of pancakes and eggs. When the smells of breakfast reached Aubree, her stomach lurched, but she forced herself to swallow and breathe slowly. She reached for the glass of milk beside the plate and took a sip. She had just picked up her fork when Haskins and the other man entered the room.

"Go ahead and eat. This won't take long," Haskins said.

Aubree put down her fork and frowned. "What kind of questions do you have for me today?"

"First, let me introduce Agent Jason Edwards from the FBI." Haskins gave a half-smile to the man dressed in a shirt and tie.

"The FBI?" Aubree's voice rose a notch.

"He's going to tell you about some new information we've discovered and how it affects you." Haskins sat in a wobbly folding chair.

Aubree stared at the FBI agent as he approached her. He carried the signature dark jacket over his arm. The sleeves of his white dress shirt were rolled up. He was lanky, but she could see the outline of his sculpted biceps. When he extended his hand to Aubree, she noticed a tattoo on his arm half-hidden by the rolled-up shirtsleeve. An orange and black flame wound around his muscle. "It's nice to meet you, Mrs. Stewart. I'm very sorry for your loss."

"Thank you. But I want to know if you've talked to my mother yet and if I can call her."

"We were able to reach her early this morning, Mrs. Stewart. We're arranging travel plans for her. She's expecting to hear from you today." He ran a hand through his short hair. It was bleached blond, and Aubree guessed him to be a native of California.

"Please call me Aubree."

"I will if you finish your breakfast, Mrs. Stewart. We're under strict orders from the doctor." He smiled at her, and Aubree sighed and picked up her fork.

He sat next to her, and Aubree could smell the fresh scent of after-shave. He dug into a briefcase and retrieved two green file folders. "This investigation is being lifted to the federal level because of what we learned early this morning," he said. "Several parts of the investigation are ongoing and cannot be discussed, but I can share a few details with you."

Aubree's heart quickened, and she took a deep breath. "The Federal level?"

"Yesterday you reported the details of a conversation. You said you heard the name 'Tidmore.'"

"Yes, he said 'Tidmore did the job,'" Aubree replied.

"Well, after the body was found and your husband was murdered, we immediately searched for any and all Tidmores." Agent Edwards clasped his hands together and looked Aubree in the eye. "We found a Charles Tidmore today. He lived about fifty miles outside of San Diego and had been murdered in his apartment."

Aubree gasped, and Haskins moved to stand beside her.

"I'm telling you this because we're concerned for your life," Agent Edwards continued. "By now you must realize that the killers have discovered that your husband was not the one who heard the conversation."

Aubree's head jerked up. "But how would they know—they killed Devin."

"We don't think this is just one person. The crimes have been committed very quickly—we think it's a team." He ran a finger along the collar of his shirt. "It would be easy for them to double-check the number they dialed against the number of the cell phone they took from your house and to discover they weren't the same." He tapped the green folders with his index finger. "We believe after they discovered this, they decided to kill Tidmore to cover their tracks."

"Are you all right?" Haskins asked.

The only thing Aubree could do was nod as she watched the remains of her breakfast getting cold.

Agent Edwards rubbed the back of his neck and frowned. "I'm sorry to upset you again, but you need to know because we consider you a witness in a triple murder investigation. We still haven't identified the body found in the manhole yet, but we're concerned that someone went to such great lengths to cover their tracks when you heard so little of the conversation."

"How can I be a witness? All I did was hear a phone call."

He hesitated and licked his lips. "Have you heard of voice recognition? It's not solid evidence, but if we brought in suspects and had them speak, you might be able to recognize the voice."

Aubree's eyes widened. "I can't put my baby in danger."

"No, we would never consider that. You would be completely protected," Agent Edwards said.

"But how? They've already killed my husband and someone else. What if they find me here?" A tense fear wound through her shoulders, and she clenched her jaw.

"You're in a private facility surrounded by security personnel. You're safe here, but you won't be able to return to your home."

"But—you mean never?" She thought of her home, of Devin, of their wedding picture hanging in the bedroom, and of the leather ottoman Devin loved to rest his feet on. So many memories interlaced with common objects.

Agent Edwards frowned. "I'm afraid it won't be safe until this case is solved. We're setting up surveillance at your home and planting a decoy there to see if the killer will try again."

Aubree's heart felt heavy as one more weight of disappointment settled on her. Agent Edwards interrupted her thoughts.

"I wanted to ask if you remember anything else about the conversation. What kind of voice did you hear? Was there any kind of background noise?"

Aubree forced herself to recall the horrifying conversation from yesterday morning that had sent her life into a tailspin.

"His voice was gruff, and he laughed when he talked about where the body was hidden. He sounded so . . ." Aubree shuddered. "So triumphant." She opened her eyes and looked at Agent Edwards.

"Can you recall any other words?"

Her shoulders slumped, but he continued. "At the time they may have seemed insignificant, but we're checking out every possibility. It may not be important that you heard a certain voice. Maybe they're after you because of a certain word or phrase you heard." He opened one of the green files and moved his finger along until it rested on a word. "I want you to replay the conversation in your mind. Put yourself back in your car, holding the phone to your ear. Listen and tell me in what context the word *intruder* was used."

With a shallow breath, Aubree closed her eyes and imagined being in her car yesterday morning. The sun had glared off of a few bug spots on her windshield, and she'd used the window wipers to clear it. She could hear the squeak of the wipers and swish of the water spraying across the windshield. Devin's ring tone was set to a Jamaican beach tune. She'd only heard a few bars before pushing "accept" on the call.

Immediately, her pulse quickened as she thought about the man saying, *Tidmore did the job, and the body is hidden in the manhole on 32nd Street.* She breathed in through her nose and tried to remember what he had said next. "He said something about the intruder."

She heard the folding chair squeak when someone moved, but she kept her eyes closed, listening and trying to piece together the fragments of her memory. The rough sound of the man's voice had eclipsed any background noise. Aubree remembered the clipped way he spoke and thought about what he had said next. She whispered, "The intruder will clear the way." When she opened her eyes, Agent Edwards was writing in the green folder as Cody and Haskins watched her.

"That was great." He stopped writing and looked at her. "If you think of anything else, anything at all, please let me know." Agent Edwards stood and shoved the folders back into his bag. He pulled a card from his back pocket and handed it to Aubree. "We're not trying to hold you hostage, Mrs. Stewart, we just don't want anyone else hurt." His phone rang, and he pulled it from the clip on his belt, lifted his head toward Aubree, and said, "I'll be back later."

Haskins handed her a bag. "Thanks for your help. We had someone pick up some maternity clothes for you. Why don't you change, and then I can take you to a phone to call your mother." Aubree looked at her hospital gown, then took the bag and glanced inside at the new clothes.

"Thank you," she whispered and hurried into the bathroom without another word. After she heard the outer door click, she turned the water on and tried to concentrate on the sound of the shower beating against the tile to rid her mind of the criminal's voice.

Her body ached, and she felt the weight of her pregnancy growing heavier with each hour. Aubree stepped into the stream of water and let the tears come again. She could have a good cry now and then maybe hold it together when she talked to her mom about Devin.

After she showered and dressed, she looked in the mirror again, tying the string on the soft green maternity blouse at the small of her back. The dainty yellow flowers on the blouse were pretty, but unfortunately no one had thought about getting her makeup, so there was nothing to disguise her splotchy face or the blonde eyelashes that rimmed her puffy eyelids.

She combed out her hair and tucked a strand behind her ear. She wondered why the police couldn't have brought some clothes and personal items from her house and then remembered it was still a crime scene. Looking at the square diamond on her finger, she thought of Devin. She tried to remember the way he would smile and laugh, but truthfully he hadn't done much of that lately.

He always tried to joke around, but Aubree had sensed a departure from his former carefree self. He worried constantly over their finances and continually urged Aubree to work "just a little longer to help make ends meet." She tried to discover what had been bothering him, but each time she probed, he would change the subject. She thought back to a conversation they'd had five months ago, when Aubree decided she wouldn't return to work after the baby was born.

"I'd like to try my hand at this stay-at-home mom business," Aubree said as Devin helped button her dress.

"Why? Don't you think you'll get bored?"

"I've been thinking about this baby." She took his hand and placed it on her abdomen. "I want to take care of our child. I don't want to miss a minute."

Devin's eyes widened. "You sure about this? Maybe you should work at least part-time."

"But we don't really need my income." She took a step away from Devin, but he pulled her back to face him.

"What?" He sounded surprised.

Aubree hesitated and then straightened her shoulders. "When I thought about becoming a mother, I knew I'd have to give up certain things." She placed a hand on Devin's arm. "I've worked hard, and we've saved like crazy. I think it would be okay for me to take a break to raise our child." She hugged Devin, and he put his arms around her. The scent of his favorite soap lingered on his skin, and Aubree inhaled and smiled.

He kissed her ear and murmured, "That's a good plan, but let's see how our finances look after the baby is born."

She pulled her face back so she could look him in the eyes. "I love you, Devin, and I love this child. I want to be a mom now, and I know I could keep working and be a mom too, but this is important to me."

Devin stared at her and shook his head. "Whatever you say, babe." Then he laughed and tickled her, and the uneasy moment had passed.

Now, as she looked into the mirror, a new realization came to her. Everything was lost—broken. Devin was gone. The family she had prepared for, worked for, saved for was no more.

"Oh, what will I do?" Aubree whispered. How could she go on without Devin? He wasn't perfect, but neither was she, and she loved him. She put her face in her hands and cried.

"Aubree, are you okay in there?"

She recognized the voice of Dr. Samuels and opened the door.

"You don't look well. Come over here and sit down."

Aubree let herself be guided back to the chair she'd sat in earlier.

Dr. Samuels held out an orange pill bottle. "I brought something for your nerves."

"I don't want to take anything. I have to be careful for my baby."

"This is a class C medication; it won't harm your baby." Dr. Samuels handed her the prescription bottle. "You need to take care of yourself. This is just enough to last you for the next few weeks."

"But I don't want to be numb to everything. I want to remember Devin." Aubree whimpered, and she wrapped her arms around herself and let the pills fall from her hand.

"Aubree, I'm trying to help you. You need to take some of this medicine and then this sedative tonight to help you sleep."

"What I need is to talk to my mother." Aubree stood slowly. "Officer Haskins said I could speak with her this morning."

"All right then. Come with me. He's actually been waiting for you to get ready." Dr. Samuels picked up the pill bottle and put it on the nightstand.

With swollen eyes, she followed Dr. Samuels out the door and down a long hallway. The facility was clean and quiet, and Aubree noticed the security guards standing at the outer doors. Dr. Samuels led her into another room filled with chairs and a phone in each corner sitting atop dark brown tables.

Officer Haskins and Detective Rawlings were in one corner, and they looked up when she entered. Cody was on the phone, scribbling something on a piece of paper while Haskins typed on a laptop—or was attempting to type. His fingers hen-pecked at the keys, and she guessed they were both working on her case. She hoped they would figure it all out so that she could go home soon.

"I want to call my mom now."

Haskins walked over to her. "The FBI has been in touch with her, and they're sending some agents to pick her up in the next hour and take her to the airport."

Aubree nodded, and Haskins handed her the phone. She gripped the receiver with trembling hands as he dialed. After only the first ring, she heard a familiar voice.

"Hello?"

"Mom." She said the word quietly and choked back the emotions waiting to erupt again.

"Aubree!" Her mom's voice sounded shaky. "It's so awful. I'm coming there as soon as I can. I only heard about it a few hours ago. I've been packing and waiting for the FBI agents to come, but then the police came over. They've been trying to collect some information about you and Devin to help with the investigation. Where are you?"

"I'm in—" Aubree started to answer when she heard a commotion, and someone grabbed the phone from her hand.

FIVE

* * *

STARTLED AND ANGRY, AUBREE looked up to see the FBI agent covering the mouthpiece on the phone. Agent Edwards' face was crimson, and it made his hair look almost white.

"I'm sorry, Mrs. Stewart. I thought someone had explained to you that you cannot share any details about your case."

"What? Give me the phone. I'm trying to talk to my mother. I'm not doing anything illegal!" Aubree shouted and stood up.

As she reached for the phone, Edwards said, "Aubree listen, the police didn't contact your mother this morning. It must've been someone else related to this crime."

"What? How did you know?"

"We have these lines tapped into a listening service," Edwards replied and pointed at the clear spiral cord trailing from his ear.

"Okay, but how could they find her so fast?"

Edwards didn't answer. He put the phone to his ear. "Hello, this is Agent Jason Edwards from the FBI. I'm sorry to interrupt your phone call, but I need to verify that you are Madeline Nelson. Can you please tell me what condition your daughter is in?"

Aubree sat silently and watched as he nodded his head. "And when is she due?" There was another pause. "What is she having? A boy or girl?" He smiled and nodded again. Then he sat beside Aubree and covered the mouthpiece. "Haskins, Cody, we need to get somebody over to Aubree's mother's home in Idaho ASAP. Some police officers went over there today."

"They couldn't have been our guys," Haskins said.

"They weren't. They were trying to see if Mrs. Nelson knows anything. Our guys weren't scheduled to pick her up for another hour."

"Consider it done. We'll have her leave immediately," Haskins said.

"Hold on a minute. I'm going to put Mrs. Nelson on speakerphone, and I want you to hear what she has to say." Edwards looked at Aubree. "You cannot tell your mother where you are. If you do, it could put her life in danger."

Aubree swallowed and reminded herself to be brave as the agent pressed the button for the speakerphone. "Mom, I'm okay."

"I wish I could be there to hold you right now," Madeline said. "I'm so sorry this happened."

"Mrs. Nelson, this is Agent Edwards again. I'd like you to be ready to leave as soon as possible. Our agents will be there to pick you up shortly, and you can take the first flight available into San Diego. I'll have someone meet you there so that you can be with your daughter."

"But where is Aubree? Are you holding her somewhere?"

Aubree leaned toward the phone. "Mom, it's all right. I didn't want to be at the house right now."

"How do you know these men are real agents?"

"Because I—"

Edwards held up his hand again. "Mrs. Nelson, I can assure you we are true officers of the law. You don't need to worry about Aubree. We're just trying to help her get some rest and keep your grandchild safe."

"But the police officers that came to my home today told me about what Devin did. They told me about the other things connected to this case, so I don't know why you're being so secretive." Madeline's voice continued to rise in pitch.

"They said that Devin was in some kind of trouble. Aubree, they said the FBI might get involved and that I should call these police officers immediately if they did because it was out of the FBI's jurisdiction."

"Mom, Devin didn't do anything. He was murdered." Aubree covered her mouth.

"I don't know who to trust," Madeline said. "Aubree, you need to get out of there. I don't think you're safe."

"Mrs. Nelson, I'm afraid those men weren't real police officers," Edwards interrupted. "Whatever you do, don't call them. In fact, I'd like you to give me the number. It's probably not even a real number," he said.

"Why should I give you the number?" Madeline demanded.

"Fine," Edwards said through gritted teeth. "Call the Federal Bureau of Investigation yourself and ask them if Jason Edwards is a legitimate officer."

"I'm sorry," Madeline said, "but they told me Aubree might be in danger and that I needed to find out where she was and contact them. Aubree, honey, they said Devin had over thirty-five thousand dollars in credit card debt from Internet gambling."

"Mom, that's not true. They weren't—"

Edwards picked up the phone before Aubree could finish. "Mrs. Nelson, I realize you're worried, but we need you to finish packing. Don't answer the door or the telephone until you see this same number on your caller ID. That will be me calling to verify that my agents are there to pick you up. At that time, I will give you a code word and when my agents show up, they'll also have identification. Aubree is under a lot of stress, and it would help her if you could get here safely and soon."

Aubree's mind was spinning as Edwards spoke to her mother. Internet gambling—she had immediately protested but suddenly felt it was true. Devin was always working on the computer, and he'd been passed up for a promotion at work because he hadn't turned in reports on time. But thirty-five thousand dollars? That part couldn't be true.

Edwards hung up the phone. The fiery tattoo moved as he flexed his arm. He frowned, and it caused his forehead to crease in several places.

"We'll be back in a bit, Edwards," Cody said as he and Haskins left the room. Each footstep reverberated against the tile and pounded against Aubree's overwhelmed mind.

"Is my mom going to be okay?"

"Yes. I think someone was trying to get information from her. I didn't want to scare her, but those men couldn't have been real police officers. We're going to check the numbers they gave her, but I doubt they'll lead anywhere. I'm sure they're planning on keeping her under surveillance. I just hope they haven't tapped into her phone already."

"But they wouldn't hurt my mom . . ." Aubree's eyes filled with tears.

Edwards handed her a tissue. "Our guys will make sure she's safe. She should be here soon."

"And then I can see her?"

"Yes, but you're still going to have to be careful. You can't divulge anything about this case to your mother, or you risk putting her in danger." He looked at her and frowned again. "After the funeral, you'll be removed to protective custody and won't be able to see anyone you know for awhile."

"But—"

"Aubree," Edwards interrupted and looked at her with a piercing gaze. "We don't want any more deaths in this case. After the incident with your mother, at the very least, we'll have to do some heavy surveillance if she is to return home."

She swallowed a lump in her throat. "It's true, isn't it?"

He raised his eyebrows.

"The gambling debt," Aubree ventured. "Devin was involved with Internet gambling." She said it as a statement of fact, because she believed it was true. Cody had given her a sympathetic glance before leaving the room. They all knew.

It didn't seem possible for Edwards to frown any deeper, but he did and then banged the table. "I'm sorry. There was no reason for you to find out like this."

"No reason?" She felt the heat rising in her cheeks. "Oh, you mean since my husband was murdered, I'm pregnant, alone, and about to be placed in a witness protection program—why make my life worse?"

Edwards wiped his hand over his face and looked at the floor. "No, I wasn't sure of all the details, and yes, I guess I didn't want to add to your burdens. I planned on checking into everything and giving you some time before . . ." he narrowed his eyes and cursed under his breath.

She leaned over the table and put her head in her hands. Her chest ached when she remembered all the times Devin had talked about her working to bring in extra money. She felt the heat of anger flushing her skin. Because of Devin's foolish gambling, he had been willing to take her away from their newborn baby to pay his debts.

She could feel Edwards watching her, and she looked up with weary eyes. "Thirty-five thousand dollars?"

He pulled out a sheet of paper from one of his green file folders and slid it across the table. "I'm afraid your husband had a problem with gambling before you even met. The thirty-five thousand is just one debt these criminals were able to find. He also had two others for ten thousand each."

Aubree's chest tightened, and she found it hard to breathe as she pulled the sheet of paper toward her. There was his name, Devin M. Stewart, above a loan in which his car had been used as collateral and later taken from him. She remembered his sad story of how he'd had to sell his car to pay for tuition, and she grimaced.

Was her entire life with Devin a lie? Who was he really? Her lip began to tremble again. "I don't know what's happening," she whispered. "My life is falling apart, and I don't even know who my husband is anymore."

Edwards popped his knuckles and his breath came out in a huff. "I'm very sorry. Gambling is a real addiction, and it looks like your husband may have been suffering from it. It doesn't make him a monster, just someone with a problem who needed help."

A few tears slipped down her cheeks and dropped onto the surface of the table. Aubree watched the tears pool together in front of her and shrugged. She was gradually seeing her life with Devin through a clearer lens. There were so many times he had acted secretive, and she had written it off as his quiet male personality. She didn't want to believe he had been hiding this huge secret—one that accrued interest daily.

She clenched her fists and gazed at the sheets of paper before her until the dollar signs started to blur. It was incredible that Devin had held it together as well as he had. He'd kept up a pretty good cover while each day, as he tried to keep it secret from her, the staggering debt must have been crushing the life out of him.

"What will happen to the debts?" Aubree asked.

"They were all in Devin's name. I don't want you to worry about them. He didn't use any of your joint assets as collateral. Focus on all the good things you knew about your husband, okay?" Edwards gave her a weak smile.

The words replayed in her head: All the good things you *knew* about your husband. What else *didn't* she know about Devin? She wrapped her arms around herself and rocked back and forth slowly as the tears continued to fall.

A nurse escorted Aubree back to her room. The emotional trauma was starting to take a toll on her. She saw the pill bottle on the nightstand, shook her head, and pushed it into a drawer. *I don't need pills! I want my life back,* she thought. As she eased onto the bed, she realized that even if Devin hadn't died, the truth about his gambling debts would've surfaced someday. The pain of his deceit compounded with the agony of his murder was too much. Her head throbbed, and she willed herself to concentrate on something besides the unraveling threads of her life.

As she lay under the crisp white sheets of the bed, she tried to shut out the questions and confusion in her mind. The second hand on the clock ticked in time with a swaying cord that hung from the blinds above the air conditioning vent. The tiny noises lulled her to sleep.

Her growling stomach brought her to her senses a few hours later. It was horrible that she could feel hungry at a time like this, but then her hand strayed to her abdomen, and she felt the firmness of her baby inside. She had to get through this for the baby. Aubree closed her eyes and whispered another prayer, a plea for help to make it through this ordeal. At least her mother would be here soon, and that thought brought a surge of comfort to her.

Her stomach continued to growl, and she sat up slowly from the bed and pushed the nurse's call button. Within seconds, there was a light knock on the door, and Haskins poked his head in.

"How can I help you?"

"You're back?" Aubree asked.

"Yes, and your mother should be here shortly," he said and pointed at the clock above Aubree's bed. She turned around, surprised to see the hour hand sitting between the four and five. She had slept the better part of the day away.

"No wonder I'm hungry. How soon will my mom be here?"

"Her flight is arriving within the next half hour. Someone will bring her here."

Cody walked in behind Haskins and pulled up a folding chair next to the bed. Aubree noticed he held a manila envelope marked "Evidence."

"Aubree, can you tell me the significance of the newspaper you requested from your home?"

Aubree's smile was bittersweet. She knew they had found the paper and must've been puzzling over the writings Devin had left.

"Every morning when Devin reads the paper, he circles names he thinks would be good for our baby. He uses a red pen and sometimes puts a star by them. I wanted to see what names he marked yesterday."

Haskins raised his eyebrows and then asked, "So he only circles names that would be good for your baby?"

"Yes."

"Well then, we may have to keep this in evidence a little longer. We're not sure if the criminal wrote on it." Cody said.

"Wait. He liked to kid around, too." She kept her eyes on the envelope. "Sometimes he would circle names of businesses because he knew it would make me laugh. Like last week he circled a Sears ad and wrote Stewart beside it."

Haskins chuckled. "Well, that explains a lot. Cody, pull out the paper—no wait."

Aubree sat up and extended her arm. "Please let me see it."

"You need to remember your husband was shot at the kitchen table. This is just a copy of the newspaper; we have to keep the original for evidence. Are you sure you want to see it?"

"Yes."

"Okay, then." Haskins motioned to Cody to hand her the paper.

He pulled out a sheaf of copies from the envelope and handed them to her. Aubree took them with shaking hands. The papers rattled and scraped against each other, and she tried to keep from gripping them too tight.

She could see several large spots on the papers. Fortunately, the copies had been done in black and white, but she still gasped and held a hand over her mouth. Haskins watched her closely, and Aubree blinked until the moisture in her eyes subsided.

She flipped through a couple before she saw the first circled name. She now understood why Haskins had been laughing. Aubree smiled and read aloud, "Chevron Stewart." Devin had written "Stewart" in big caps letters with an exclamation point beside it. The ad was for a grand opening for the new gas station in town.

"You can see why we were concerned. We wondered if it was some kind of code," Haskins said as he sat back in his chair.

"You can keep this copy. I'm very sorry for all you're going to have to go through, but we'll do our best to solve this case." Cody stood, offering his hand.

"Thank you." Aubree shook Cody's hand and nodded at Haskins.

"We'll see you later. I'll tell someone to bring your meal." Cody waved as he exited the room. "And don't worry, we've got someone watching this door at all times."

"Thank you," she said again, but this time she remembered that the police still considered her life in danger. She looked at the pile of papers in her hands and blinked away oncoming tears. Wiping her eyes, she focused on the black and white pages to see what else Devin had circled.

Sorting through the papers, she smiled at other funny names Devin had marked. She flipped over another page and then stopped. In the bottom right-hand corner, there were two names circled beside each other. Devin had written in small letters in the margin, "If it's a boy" with an arrow pointing to one and "If it's a girl" with an arrow pointing to the other. The names were Joshua and Scarlett.

Aubree rubbed her stomach and whispered, "Your daddy wants to know if you like the name Joshua or Scarlett?" She felt a rhythmic movement and looked at her stomach. She smiled at the slight up-and-down pulse. The baby must have been excited over the names because he or she had hiccups.

Folding the copies of the newspaper carefully, Aubree tucked them into her purse and headed for the bathroom to freshen up. At least one memory of Devin would not be tainted by the investigation.

Haskins entered a few minutes later carrying a dinner tray overflowing with food. "I saw the nurse with your tray, so I thought I'd bring this in and see if you needed anything else."

"I'm feeling a little better now." Aubree sat in the chair beside the bed. He placed the tray of steaming mashed potatoes, gravy, and chicken in front of her. "Thank you very much." Picking up her fork, she swirled the mashed potatoes in the gravy.

"Should be just right for an Idaho gal," Haskins said as he opened the door to leave. "I'll be right here if you need anything."

Aubree nodded. "Nothing beats an Idaho potato." She smiled and took a bite of the creamy mountain.

She ate her meal slowly and tried to concentrate only on the food and not the circumstances. When she finished, she looked at the clock, wishing away the minutes until her mother would arrive. She got up and paced around the room a few times, and then she sat down again. She had never been very good at waiting.

What if there was more to Devin's murder than the wrong number? Aubree sat on the edge of the bed and traced the pattern in the blanket as she thought. What if someone was trying to collect on another gambling debt? She shook her head, ashamed at what her mom must think of Devin.

It had been nearly six months since she'd seen her mom. She and Devin traveled to Idaho to give her mother the good news that they were expecting. The trip was a joyful time, and the only sad moments were when they reflected on how excited Aubree's father would have been to meet his new grandchild.

Her father had passed away nearly four years ago from heart failure. Aubree wondered for the first time if her Dad would have approved of Devin. Would he have sensed Devin was hiding things? Aubree was disappointed in herself as she remembered her Dad's admonitions to enjoy life but to keep her eyes wide open so she could always see what was really happening. She promised herself she would do better now and hoped that somehow she could get through this mess.

Aubree walked toward the door and opened it to see Haskins sitting in a folding chair, looking at some files. "Excuse me. I wanted to know if Devin's family has been contacted."

"I'm sorry. I forgot to tell you earlier that we spoke with them late last night." He stood and stretched, then continued. "They're planning on coming to the funeral tomorrow."

"Tomorrow?" Aubree said. "I had no idea it would be so soon."

"Uh—with everything going on with the investigation, we're keeping Devin's funeral under tight security."

"But aren't I supposed to help somehow? Pick out the—" Aubree closed her mouth and squeezed her eyes shut.

"The casket?" Haskins frowned. "I'm sorry this is all so chaotic. Someone was supposed to bring some stuff by for you to look at. But it's probably been misplaced in the shuffle." Haskins offered his arm to Aubree. "Why don't we walk down the hall and see if we can find some information for you."

She nodded and took Haskins' arm. She knew this was real, but it was so horrible that it was like living a nightmare.

"Part of the problem is the FBI will be handling the major details of the case from here on out. They'll have a specialist to work with you— might be Agent Edwards."

Aubree raised her eyebrows and gave him a confused glance.

Haskins swallowed. "I think you'll be briefed on some new information soon."

"Oh." She didn't even want to imagine what else the police could've discovered that she needed to know.

She followed Haskins the rest of the way down the hall without saying anything. They picked up a packet of information from a local funeral home, and Aubree gripped it tightly and shook her head when Haskins asked her if she wanted someone to go through it with her. She returned to her room and looked at the details of Devin's funeral.

The California Bureau of Investigation had helped to arrange everything. All she had to do was mark which casket and lining she wanted and check off a few more questions. There were a few fliers on bereavement and a local support group that Aubree looked over and then tossed into the garbage. If she were to be placed in a witness protection program, she wouldn't be able to talk about her former life with Devin. A heavy weight descended on her, and for the hundredth time in the last twenty-four hours, she swallowed a lump of tears.

The click of the door handle startled her, and she looked up and wiped her eyes as her mother entered the room.

"Aubree!" Madeline Nelson dropped her bags and ran to her daughter. She crouched beside Aubree's chair and hugged her.

Somewhere in the midst of tears and heaving sobs, Aubree was able to get one word out. "Mom."

After Aubree once again drained her reservoir of tears, she held the packet of funeral information out to her mom.

"When your father died, I hoped it would be a long time before I had to attend another funeral for a family member." Madeline wiped her eyes with a tissue.

At age fifty-seven, Madeline Nelson was still a striking woman. The reddish-blonde hair Aubree had inherited from her was now a lovely white, and she had the same clear blue eyes as her daughter.

Madeline looked through the fliers and sank onto a folding chair.

"Honey, I don't know how, but you're going to get through this." She still held herself as she always had, with a commanding posture and confident air. Even through her tear-stained wrinkles, she exuded strength, and Aubree planned to cling to that for all she was worth.

"Mom, they're going to put me in a witness protection program."

"I know. An FBI agent briefed me on the way from the airport."

"They told you everything?" Aubree raised her eyebrows.

"No. I'm not supposed to ask you too many questions either. But in any case, I'm here now, and I want to help you." She straightened the papers in her lap and once more tried to focus. "Devin was fond of this type of wood, wasn't he." She pointed to a dark mahogany casket Aubree had also been looking at.

"That's pretty. Do you think this material would be good?" She stopped and put a hand over her mouth—not wanting to believe she was having this conversation with her mother. It was horrible, but there was no avoiding it. Either she would be part of her husband's funeral, or she wouldn't. Even though Devin had deceived her, she still felt she knew him better than anyone else.

They finalized all the funeral details, and then Aubree told her mom what she could about the day before. Edwards had counseled her on the importance of leaving out fine details like Tidmore's name and connections with a uniform. He said her mother could be approached again and unknowingly provide evidence that might help the killer.

"Mom, I think the FBI knows more about the case, and they're trying to decide how much to tell me. I got the idea from Officer Haskins that they might brief me later."

"Sweetie, you've got to do what they tell you. You have to keep yourself and my grandchild safe," Madeline said.

"I know, but it's so bizarre. It seems like they should be able to figure things out before I have to go somewhere else to have my baby. I wish I could come and stay with you."

"That's what I said, but the Agent—I think his name is Edwards—pointed out that the men who came to my house were not officers of the law, but criminals." Madeline squeezed her hands together. "If they could find me that fast, they must have ample resources."

Aubree pictured her mother's home in rural Idaho, twenty miles from the nearest grocery store. It was unbelievable that they'd found her so easily, and Aubree was thankful her mom hadn't been harmed. It was hard to imagine that so much could happen, that so many lives could be placed in danger, from just one wrong number.

SIX

* * *

IT WAS NEARLY SEVEN o'clock when a nurse entered the room, pulling an extra hospital bed. "This is for your mom."

"Thank you very much," Aubree said.

"We thought you'd appreciate that, Mrs. Nelson," Edwards said as he entered the room. "Being in a private care facility does have a few perks."

"Oh, thanks. You're a dear," Madeline said.

"It's not the Hilton, but you'll be safe here until some of this blows over." He fumbled with a manila envelope in his hand as if considering what to say. "The funeral is scheduled for tomorrow at eleven o'clock, but you'll both have to be briefed before then."

"Why?" Aubree asked.

Edwards motioned to Madeline. "Because she knows more than we're letting anyone else know. We need this to look like a robbery gone bad. We're all working non-stop on leads, but we can't let the press get hold of this until we have more information."

"When are you going to tell me what you *do* know?" Aubree folded her arms.

Edwards cleared his throat and gave her a crooked smile. "That's what I was coming to do." He motioned to the door. "Mrs. Nelson, if you'll come out here, we have another agent waiting to brief you on the details of the funeral. We have to be careful of what's said to protect everyone. We don't want you to mention you were contacted at home by the perpetrator."

Aubree shivered involuntarily, thinking of the perpetrator who was now her enemy. For that was what he, or they, was—the worst kind of enemy anyone could dream up.

"It'll be all right. I'm sure they're just being overly cautious." Madeline bent down to hug her daughter.

"I'll see you in a bit," Aubree said. "I'm so sorry all of this happened."

"It's not your fault. Now don't worry yourself anymore. I'm glad to be with you." Madeline carried the baby blanket she had been crocheting with her as she exited the room.

Edwards sat in the folding chair Madeline had occupied. "I wanted to tell you that the FBI has taken a major interest in this case. You'll be seeing a lot more agents and the local police will still help, but Officer Haskins and Detective Rawlings probably won't be around much."

"Oh." Aubree felt disappointed she wouldn't be seeing Officer Haskins' kind face anymore. Agent Edwards rolled up the sleeves of his dress shirt, and Aubree stared at the tattoo winding around his arm. The flame was dark orange against his tanned forearms. The hair on his arms and head was sun bleached. She glanced at his green eyes, absent of smile lines. He was all business, and Aubree wished she could escape from the details of her case.

A shadow flickered back and forth across the room, and she glanced at the window. The shade was pulled halfway, and she could see tree branches swaying in the wind, interrupting the dull light of her room.

Agent Edwards rubbed his thumb against the edge of his notebook; the shuffling sound seemed to keep time with Aubree's nervous heart rate. She glanced at the pile of green file folders in his lap and then back at him.

He opened his mouth, closed it again, and cleared his throat. "Everything I tell you has to be kept in strict confidence. You will not share any information with your mother, and you should know your room is under surveillance."

"As in video?"

"And microphone," Edwards said. "It's not because we don't trust you—that's how the room is set up in this facility."

Aubree tried not to feel defensive, but she was failing. "So I'm basically being held here like a criminal?"

"No, this is the CBI, remember? I want you to understand that everything you are going through is for your protection."

"Yeah, I'm sure it's for my own good." She looked toward the window again, wishing that she could enjoy the sunshine on a carefree day.

Edwards furrowed his brow. "As a matter of fact, it is. The case you're involved in has been upped to a level of national security."

"What!" Aubree sat up straighter in her chair and bumped her drink on the meal table. Edwards caught it before it spilled.

"I can't believe what a mess I'm in." She put her head in her hands and took a deep breath.

Edwards tapped the files with his fingers and cleared his throat again. He rubbed his hand over his hair, which was cut nearly to a buzz. He met her gaze, and now she noticed worry lines around his eyes.

"Last night we placed a decoy in your home to see if anyone came around. But no one did. By this afternoon, when no one had even driven by your house, we were beginning to feel like maybe we'd overreacted." Edwards held up his hand before Aubree could agree. "But then we discovered the identity of the person we found in the manhole."

Aubree's shoulders slumped. "So because of who this person is, I'm still not safe?"

"Yes. The identity of this person has us worried about the funeral tomorrow and your safety."

"Can you tell me who it was?" She clasped her hands together.

"That has to do with this briefing. We found him because of the information you gave us."

"His uniform?"

"We collected information on all missing persons in the last twenty-four hours and narrowed it down to only those who wore a uniform of some kind." Edwards flipped open a file and showed her a picture of a huge naval aircraft carrier.

Aubree leaned forward and examined the photo. "The USS *Midway*?"

"So you've been there?"

"Devin and I went last summer." Aubree winced when she said Devin's name, but she let the memory wash over her. They had spent a few hours at the retired aircraft carrier-turned-museum in San Diego Bay. It had been exciting to see inside a real aircraft carrier because her dad had served in the navy. Dozens of cramped stairwells winding throughout the belly of the carrier had made the deck of the *Midway* even more appealing when they had climbed to the top of the sun scorched airstrip.

"But they don't have uniforms there, do they?" Aubree tried to remember, but she didn't think the retired naval officers who had helped guide some of the tours had all looked the same. It was a busy place, though. She remembered hearing that the flagship of Desert Storm had about three million tourists per year.

Edwards pulled out a few more pictures of the *Midway*. "No, several of the guides wear the same hats and a polo shirt with USS *Midway* emblems, but the uniformed person missing was head of the night security watch." He tapped his foot and looked at Aubree. "We wondered why anyone would feel the need to murder a security guard at a popular tourist attraction. Then we realized it may coincide with a special visit from the secretary of defense. He's planning on visiting the naval carrier on Friday—that's tomorrow."

"How would killing a security guard get them close to the secretary of defense?" Aubree rubbed the back of her neck. "Are you sure my case is connected to all of this and not to Devin's gambling?"

"We asked the same question. And we've come to the conclusion that Devin's gambling didn't have anything to do with his murder." Edwards opened his briefcase and took out a few files. "Remember how I told you one word could be very important from the conversation you heard?"

Aubree nodded.

"You heard the word *intruder*, which by itself was a bit puzzling, but when we added it to the security guard at the USS *Midway*, we came up with something different."

Edwards pulled out a map that displayed airplanes of different shapes and sizes and pointed to a picture of a jet. "This is an A-6 Intruder on the flight deck of the USS *Midway*. It sits right in front of the Island Superstructure, the tower housing the bridge and primary flight control."

"I remember climbing up there during the tour to see all the controls," Aubree said. They had waited twenty minutes for their tour. The inside of the tower was hot, and Aubree recalled wiping sweat from her forehead and fanning herself with a map of the *Midway*.

"Secretary of defense, Robert Walden, will be delivering an address in front of the Island Superstructure tomorrow. He'll be standing next to the A-6 Intruder." Edwards tapped the picture, and Aubree's breath caught in her throat. The voice from the phone call repeated in her mind: *The Intruder will clear the way.*

Edwards lowered his voice and continued. "We called in our police dogs and, in conjunction with the bomb squad, they discovered an explosive hidden in the Intruder on the deck of the ship."

Aubree covered her mouth for a moment before speaking. "They were going to assassinate the secretary of defense? But why?"

Now Edwards didn't look so confident. "We don't know yet. Perhaps it was some left-wing, anti-war group. We're searching the chatter to see if any organizations are discussing plans involving the secretary of defense."

"I think I did hear something about him coming. A lot of people will be there, right? Is he still going to come?" Aubree asked.

Edwards nodded and rapped the file folders with his knuckles. "They're taking all threats into consideration, but I think he'll still give a speech. The Secret Service would've swept the entire carrier before his arrival, but I doubt they would've found the bomb in time without this lead. It took hours to find and dismantle it."

"So you've foiled their plan. I should be safe now, right?" Aubree gave him a hopeful glance.

Edwards chewed on his bottom lip and shook his head. "We don't know why they wanted to kill him. We don't know who they are. You aren't safe yet." He touched her arm gently. "I want you to know we aren't going to put you in even the smallest degree of danger. Every loose end has to be tied up, and until then, you'll be in protective custody. There's a good chance this is why they killed Devin and Tidmore, but we'll have to wait and see."

Aubree swallowed hard and blinked back tears. "Okay."

"That's all you need to know right now. Try to get some rest." Edwards stood and walked to the door. He paused before he turned the handle as if he were going to say more, but then he sighed. Aubree watched the door close behind him and listened to the clock ticking again.

✳ ✳ ✳

Agent Jason Edwards walked down the hall of the private facility. He hadn't told Aubree Stewart everything, because he didn't want to scare her into a state of shock. He didn't tell her she definitely was not safe in the slightest degree or that he was more worried for her life than he let on. Because now he had a suspicion he couldn't shake.

Her house had been too quiet—no one had come by. Even with the decoy in plain sight, no one had visited. No one had tried to delve into her personal identity; the FBI had used special Internet tracking programs to trace all of her online accounts. He was pretty sure he knew the reason. No one had tried to check up on Aubree Stewart because whoever was behind this plot already knew exactly where she was and everything about her.

SEVEN

* * *

How can the sun shine today? Aubree thought. The black dress stretched tightly over her body, soaking up the heat. The back of her neck beaded with sweat. Murmurs of comfort from others were muffled by the anxiety she felt.

Devin's funeral was sparsely attended because of the FBI's stipulations. Aubree knew it would've been that way anyway, because she and Devin didn't have many close connections in San Diego. Some of their neighbors came, but they didn't know Devin very well. All the same, Aubree was grateful for the support. Madeline stayed close to her side the entire time, fielding uncomfortable questions and keeping the visits to a minimum.

Though the whole ordeal only took a few hours, it felt like days to Aubree. The fear for her future was a distraction from the pain, and she couldn't concentrate on the changing tide of her life. She felt like a dishcloth that had been wrung out too many times, the fabric thin with fraying edges.

When Edwards escorted Aubree and Madeline to the cemetery, she noticed several undercover agents filtering through the crowd with earpieces trailing down their shirt collars. The sun illuminated the bright white of the lilies on Devin's casket, but in a few hours they would be wilting from the heat—they would resemble the state of her life.

When she returned to the private care facility, the halls were quiet, and Aubree felt like she was walking through a fog. Madeline hugged her and rubbed her aching back. "It's probably best if you rest now, dear."

"I know, Mom, but I feel so empty," Aubree said. "I tried to pay attention—to absorb these last details of Devin, but my mind kept wandering to everything he's going to miss. Everything I'm going to miss."

"I did the same thing at your father's funeral." Madeline squeezed her daughter's shoulders. "It's tough, and there's no way around it, but after a time I came to realize he would want me to be happy."

Aubree shook her head fiercely. "How will I ever be happy? My life is over! I don't even know when I'll be able to see you again."

Madeline put a hand on Aubree's stomach. "Your life is just beginning. I know you can't do it now, but before this baby is born, you have to give yourself permission to feel joy again. In so many ways, my life began when I became a mother. Devin wouldn't want you to cheat yourself from happiness, and he would want you to be happy for this child."

"I don't know what to do." Aubree held tightly to her mom and tried to find comfort in the embrace.

"Sweetie, I don't know what you're going to do either. But I do know it will work out. You're so much stronger than me, and I'm so proud of you." She squeezed Aubree tighter. "I love you."

Aubree slept fitfully for most of the afternoon, and Madeline did her best to keep her comfortable. When the nurse brought in supper, she also turned on the television.

"Agent Edwards said you might want to see this." She found the station she was looking for and then left the room.

Aubree stared at the gigantic berth of the USS *Midway* on screen. A television reporter spoke about the history of the aircraft carrier and the importance of the visit taking place within the hour.

Pretty much every airplane the aircraft carrier had ever held and then some was on deck. The reporter talked about F-14 Tomcats, C-1 Traders, FA-18 Hornets, T-2 Buckeye and others Aubree didn't recognize. The *Midway* had experienced a forty-seven–year odyssey that spanned the end of World War II to Desert Storm before it became the first museum of its kind.

The reporter said something about Secretary Walden's visit, and Aubree noticed the large crowds of people on deck as she listened. "He will be speaking about the need to continue ridding the world of nuclear weapons and about a special military-grade fuel to be produced by new ethanol plants." The reporter motioned to the podium. "He's been working closely with the secretary of agriculture on the new ethanol program, and they hope to launch it next year."

"So, it couldn't be an anti-war group—they'd support him," Aubree mumbled.

"What was that, dear?" Madeline asked.

"Oh, nothing. Just thinking about when Devin and I visited the *Midway*."

"I remember you telling me about that. Your father would've enjoyed it." Madeline smiled at Aubree and then continued writing in the notebook she had been scribbling in for the past hour. Aubree wasn't sure what her mom was doing but figured it had something to do with their impending separation.

Edwards had informed them that Aubree would be entering protective custody in a different location within the next week and that their time would be limited. For the thousandth time, she wished her mother could be there when the baby was born. Maybe they could find a way for Madeline to visit a secure location.

Aubree's attention was brought back to the TV when the secretary of defense stood up. She could see part of the wing of the Intruder overshadowing him. He spoke clearly into the microphone,

"Most of you know I've come to talk today about nuclear weapons, but I also wanted to introduce the latest plans we are working on for a greener earth and a greener economy. The Pentagon reports that the Department of Defense burns through three hundred thousand barrels of oil a day to function. We need to cut back on the use of foreign oil and rely on our own natural resources. Our nation has the capability to create cleaner, more efficient fuel sources."

The secretary of defense paused and looked out over the crowd, and then his brow furrowed. Aubree watched the screen and noticed a scuffle near some of the spectators. The camera changed views to show several people running, and then Aubree heard loud noises. Screaming and a quick report of gunfire sounded in the background. The camera was zooming in and out erratically.

"Was that a gunshot?" Madeline jumped from her chair and stood closer to the TV as Aubree turned up the volume.

Mass confusion erupted on the deck of the *Midway*. The reporter tried to speak as she was jostled about by people running in a panic.

Police officers and FBI agents swarmed the crowds, and Aubree noticed several dogs wearing police vests. The footage cut out, and it took a few minutes for the local news station to connect with the reporter on deck again.

Aubree held her breath when the camera focused in on the reporter. The woman had moved away from the confusion. Her hair fell around her face, and her makeup was smeared. She spoke rapidly and gripped the microphone with white fingers.

"There has just been an assassination attempt on Secretary Walden. We've been told that a man forced his way through the security checkpoints, firing semi-automatic weapons and killing two police officers. Shots were fired here, the gunman was killed, but Secretary Walden has been shot." The reporter looked at the crowd dispersing, and the cameraman attempted to find a good angle for the television viewers to witness the chaos.

Aubree and Madeline watched paramedics and other officials scrambling on deck as crowds of people tried to exit the *Midway*. Aubree's stomach churned with anxiety. The criminals had still tried to carry out their plan to destroy Robert Walden. How did they know the bomb wouldn't go off? She swung her legs over the side of the bed and took a few steps toward the door.

"Where are you going?" Madeline hurried to her side and grabbed her arm.

"I've got to find Agent Edwards. If they can't even keep the secretary of defense safe, how will they keep me safe?"

"Wait a minute. This is connected to Devin's murder?" Madeline's eyes widened and her face paled.

"It's okay, Mom. I'm sure the FBI can explain it to us." Aubree pursed her lips as she swung the door open and then cried out when she nearly ran into Edwards. "What is going on?"

"Aubree, we have to move you right now." He stepped into the room and closed the door.

"But I thought I wasn't leaving until next week." Aubree's hands shook, and she grabbed hold of her mom.

"I know, but this case just spontaneously combusted, and I want you out of here before you come into contact with any of the fallout." Edwards frowned and shook his head. "I'm sorry. We don't know what these people are capable of. It doesn't look good for Secretary Walden."

Aubree felt her throat tighten, and her eyes stung with moisture. "Is he going to die?"

Edwards pressed his lips into a thin line. "I don't know yet."

Madeline's bracelets jangled as she wrung her hands. "That's awful." Then she looked at Aubree, and a mask of resolve appeared on her face. "I'll help get her things together," Madeline said. "Give us a couple minutes."

"That's all we have. I'm going to be driving you myself." He opened the door. "I'll wait right here."

As soon as the door closed, Aubree wanted to crumple into a heap of tears, but the urgency in Edwards' voice drove her forward.

"Mom, I thought we'd have more time. I don't know if I can do this alone."

"You won't be alone. This is all going to be over soon. I just know it." Madeline stuffed her notebook inside a bag with a few other belongings for Aubree. "Go use the bathroom before you leave, and I'll put some snacks in here for you."

Aubree hurried into the bathroom and tried to calm her racing heart. She could feel the blood pulsing in her neck, and she took a couple deep breaths. She grabbed the few toiletry items she'd been given and scanned the sterile bathroom, then hurried out the door and grabbed her purse from the bedside table. It was the only thing that was really hers.

"What's going to happen to all of my things and to my house?"

Madeline handed Aubree a tissue. "I spoke to someone yesterday. We're packing everything up, and you're moving. The FBI is taking care of everything. I'm having them put your things in storage."

Tears trickled down Aubree's cheek, and she wiped at them angrily. "I'm going to lose everything." She thought about her photo albums, pictures of Devin, her journals—it felt like her whole life was being taken from her.

"No, it will be here when you get back," Madeline said. "You won't lose Devin's things."

Aubree hugged her mom. It was wonderful how her mom always knew what she was thinking. "Mom, I'm going to do everything I can to stay in touch with you."

"Be safe, Aubree. That's the only thing that matters. Be safe and be smart and take care of yourself and my grandbaby." She hugged her. "I love you."

The door opened, and Edwards stepped inside. Aubree saw the worry lines creasing his face.

"I love you too, Mom." Aubree squeezed Madeline's hand and headed for the door.

Edwards picked up the bag and shook Madeline's hand. "I'll keep her safe," he said.

"I know you will." Madeline wiped at the tears running down her cheeks.

"This way." He motioned for Aubree to come with him. She kept her head down and swallowed the tears stuck in her throat, following Edwards' quick strides out of the facility in silence. He helped her into a dark sedan and closed the door. Aubree felt he was closing the door on her life.

His cell phone rang, and he answered it as he put the car into drive. He cursed and then hung up. "Secretary Walden didn't make it."

"They killed him?"

Edwards nodded and turned on the radio as they drove away from the facility. All the stations were broadcasting news about the attempted assassination on the USS *Midway*; they didn't know yet that it was more than just an attempt.

"How did that man get past your checkpoints?" Aubree asked. "I thought nobody got assassinated anymore."

Edwards breathed heavily, and his lips protruded as he moved his tongue over his teeth. "I'm not sure how to handle this situation. I don't want to scare you, but, then again, I do because I want you to see how serious this is." He glanced at her and continued, "No one knew we had found the bomb on the *Midway*, but the gunman was sent to kill Secretary Walden because *they* knew."

"Who is *they*?" Aubree whispered.

"I don't know, but whoever they are, they had help on the inside today. Somehow the information about the bomb was leaked to them, and they sent someone to do damage control." He stopped at a red light and turned to Aubree. "They wanted the secretary of defense dead, and they didn't care how many casualties piled up in the process. I don't know if you're still a threat to them, but we can't take any chances."

"But do you really think they'd come after me now? Secretary Walden is dead, and I can't identify anyone."

Aubree saw Edwards' muscles tense, and the tattoo on his arm rippled with the movement. "I'm taking you to a special FBI house that is deep undercover. I'm hoping we'll be able to decipher what kind of a threat you are to these people while you're there."

"How long will I have to stay there?" Aubree clasped her hands together.

"As long as we need to make sure you're safe." Edwards glanced at her hands on her stomach. "You might want to rest for a bit. We'll be driving for a few more hours."

"How far are we going?"

Edwards shook his head, and she slumped back into the seat and closed her eyes. She wanted to ask more questions, but doubted he would answer. She felt overwhelmed with the information he'd already given her. If only she could figure out what someone thought she knew, some piece of information that was worth killing for.

"Let me know if you need anything," Edwards whispered.

✳ ✳ ✳

Edwards watched Aubree settle into her seat and shift her growing pregnancy to a more comfortable position. His eyes were moist with the concern he felt for her. She was only a couple months from delivering her first baby, and here she was entering protective custody. He gritted his teeth.

As he drove, he wished he could get inside her head and hear a recording of the voice that started all the chaos. He couldn't help but wonder if the voice would belong to someone who had a high profile—someone with a lot of money to lose if anyone ever connected him to this case. Someone who had also infiltrated the highest area of law enforcement—the FBI.

EIGHT

✳   ✳   ✳

WHEN AUBREE WOKE, SHE felt disoriented, but it only took her a second to remember why she was riding in a car with an FBI agent. She squeezed her eyes shut again and thought about Devin. She felt the baby moving and mouthed the names Devin had circled in the newspaper—Joshua and Scarlett. She opened her eyes again and adjusted her seat so she could see out the window.

"Do you need anything?" Edwards asked.

Aubree shook her head. "Where are we?" The noise of traffic was a dull roar outside of the car, and red taillights dotted the horizon, glaring at her through the blackness of the night.

"We're almost there. We're on the outskirts of Los Angeles."

Aubree saw the green numbers on the dashboard clock change to 9:07. They had been driving for nearly three hours. She stretched her legs as best she could and sat up straighter in her seat. "Agent Edwards, I need to use the bathroom."

"Why don't you call me Jason? Looks like we're going to be spending some time together," he said. "Only about fifteen more minutes. I'm sorry. I'm sure you're uncomfortable."

"Well, hopefully in about eight weeks, I won't be so uncomfortable anymore."

He chuckled. "We'll have a doctor come to the house for your check-ups. It's too risky to go to your regular doctor."

Aubree tried not to think how it was just one more bit of normalcy gone from her life. She squinted to view her surroundings out the window, but it was too dark. Then they turned into a neighborhood with street lamps on every corner that illuminated three-story, picturesque houses with neatly manicured lawns. Within a few minutes, she felt the car slow down, and Jason pulled into a circular driveway in front of a two-story rambler.

"Hold on a minute," he said and jumped out of the car.

Aubree watched him punch in numbers on a keypad, which opened the double garage door. He hurried back and pulled the car in slowly. "Let me close the garage before you get out." She pulled her hand back from the door and waited. A few seconds later, he opened her door, and she followed him into the house.

Once inside, they stopped again as he entered a code into another keypad and slid some kind of card through a slot on a thick steel door. The keypad beeped, and Jason turned the handle. Aubree felt nervous as she followed him inside the spacious home. Right beside the kitchen, a small office filled with various kinds of electronic equipment caught her eye, and then her heart jumped as a huge man walked around the corner.

"Hey, Sanderson. Glad to see you again." Jason shook the hand of a man who had to be at least six and a half feet tall. He wore dark blue jeans and a white polo shirt, which contrasted with the dark skin on his shaved head. Aubree could see tufts of curly black hair escaping from the opening on his shirt.

He smiled broadly and held out a large hand. "Garrett Sanderson, FBI."

She reached a trembling hand forward, all the time cursing herself for being such a scaredy-cat. "I'm Aubree Stewart."

"So, it's the informant on the Walden case." A tall brunette walked into the kitchen. "I'm Miranda Olsen."

"I didn't know you were on shift here," Jason said. Aubree noticed a bit of impatience in his voice.

"For the rest of the month." Miranda winked and opened the fridge. "Are you hungry, Aubree?"

"A little."

"We don't cook a lot, but I made some chicken stir-fry earlier, if you'd like some." Miranda pulled out a covered dish and set it on the counter.

"That would be fine." Aubree felt completely out of place among all the FBI agents.

"Why don't you come this way while Agent Olsen gets that ready, and I'll show you around." Jason carried her bag down a hallway that opened up to two large bedrooms. "This is a master bed and bath."

The oversized room held a huge cherry wood sleigh bed and was decorated in shades of blue matching the plush azure carpet. The bathroom adjoining it was also enormous, with a Jacuzzi tub, a separate shower, and a walk-in closet. "It's nice," she said, as she ran her hand along a sleek cherry wood desk. There was a television, a radio, and a computer set up in the room.

"I hope you'll be comfortable here. Tomorrow I'll show you the garden out back. It's all enclosed and really beautiful." Jason paused in the doorway. "Everyone is working around the clock—this case just moved to the number one position. We're trying to get your life back."

She slipped off her sandals, and her toes sank into the carpet. Looking at her feet, Aubree murmured, "I know."

"Oh, I almost forgot." Jason pulled something out of his briefcase. "This was from the funeral today." He handed her a picture frame. "I thought you might want it."

She reached out for the silver frame, which held an enlarged photo of Devin. Her breath caught in her throat when she looked at his carefree smile. She met Jason's eyes and nodded, then turned away before the tears escaped down her cheeks.

NINE

* * *

SIX WEEKS LATER IN early November, a light breeze ruffled the edge of Aubree's yellow maternity shirt. She was anything but comfortable as she sat in a deck chair with her hands resting on her swollen stomach, but the gardens were beautiful.

The backyard of the safe house was completely enclosed by a fence covered in flowering vines and also by a canopy of mature trees. Every day, Aubree spent a few hours outside reading and resting amid the gorgeous landscaping that was complete with a gurgling stream and Koi fish. She enjoyed listening to the running water, allowing it to fill her head and block out the painful memories that were still too fresh.

The face of her husband surfaced in her dreams each night, but during the day she had to look at his picture several times to remind herself of the fine details. She wrote in her journal, *I don't want to forget Devin. I just want to forget the secrets he kept from me.* It was difficult to feel the pain of losing her husband at the same time she had to deal with the confusion of his deceit.

After she discovered the truth about his gambling addiction, Aubree had hoped his death was related to his problem, but the FBI continued to assure her there was no connection. It would've been a much simpler case to solve. Instead, she was forced to wait as the FBI checked the validity of every new lead and tip on the assassination of Secretary Walden.

A pile of papers held down by a large rock fluttered in the breeze. They were notes Aubree had written of every scrap of memory she could come up with about the wrong number she'd received a call from. It drove her crazy that there were parts of the conversation she couldn't remember.

Sketches of the inside of her car did nothing to restore her memory. Picking up the pages, she glanced over her notes again, the ones she'd written about the sensory details of that brief phone call. The hum of her car idling at the stoplight, the radio playing softly, a clicking noise from inside one of the air vents—all of these sounds set the stage and increased her blood pressure.

She closed her eyes and put herself back in the car. *Tidmore did the job, and the body is hidden in the manhole on 32nd Street . . .* , and then he'd said something about the Intruder. She squeezed her eyes tight and remembered the car behind her at the stoplight; the bass had been turned up so loud it reverberated in her chest. A horn blared, but that was later after he said, *Hey, don't I at least get a congrats? What's up with you? I even kept his uniform for you.* Aubree exhaled slowly and whispered, "What else did he say?"

"Aubree, I told you to quit beating yourself up over that," Jason said.

Her eyes flew open. "You scared me!" she shrieked.

"Sorry." Jason plopped in a deck chair and tossed an orange up and down in the air. "You're scaring me. You're stressing out over that conversation too much."

Aubree raised her eyebrows. "So first you guys drive me crazy trying to get me to remember every detail, and then you tell me I'm stressing out over it."

He ran a hand over his buzz cut. "I think it's time for you to take a break. Give it a rest and concentrate on getting that baby here." Jason handed her the orange. "We'll take care of your case."

She brought the orange to her nose and sniffed it. "Hmm, I wish I could give it a rest." The juice ran down her fingers as she peeled the orange. "I wish *I* could rest. The nightmares make it so I don't want to fall asleep."

Jason leaned forward in his chair. "I'm sorry, but I really want you to give it a rest for now. Please, don't worry about this anymore until after the baby is born."

"But I want to help so you can solve my case."

"We're going to solve your case." He covered her hand with his. "You've done great. I don't want you to worry anymore right now."

Aubree nodded and looked down at Jason's hand. "I'll try to rest."

"That's my girl." He patted her hand. "I'd better get back to work."

Chewing slowly on an orange slice, Aubree watched Jason reenter the house and tried to quiet the voices in her head. She didn't want to rest anymore. She wanted to get on with her life and leave the horrible feelings surrounding Devin's murder behind, but she couldn't do that until the FBI said she was safe.

The notebook from her mother lay open on the picnic table. Madeline had written several notes and cheerful letters including some of her favorite thoughts and snippets of poems. Aubree flipped through the pages to find one of the letters in order to get her mind off of unpleasant thoughts. Madeline encouraged Aubree to fill a journal with good things about Devin and advised her, *Forgive Devin his past and prepare to live a life that isn't empty because of the loss of your husband but full because of the child yet to come.*

It was easier said than done, but she knew her mom spoke from experience. She stood and walked toward the shade of a nearby tree.

Adjusting her sunglasses against the California sun, Aubree thought about her doctor's appointment a few days ago. Over the past week, she'd been having Braxton Hicks contractions, and her abdomen felt sore from all the cramping.

"I'm tired of all these false alarms," Aubree complained to the doctor.

He chuckled and wrote a few notes in her chart. "Braxton Hicks are pretty common. Don't worry, you have two weeks left, but you're looking good, and the baby could come any time."

Time. The only sure way she could measure her life right now was by the amount of time she spent in hiding. Six weeks already, and no end in sight. The fish drifted up and down the little stream feeding into the larger pond, and Aubree thought she knew what they felt like. They could swim all day, but they weren't getting anywhere.

On his way to grab supplies, Jason stopped by the patio window and watched Aubree walk slowly around the garden area, the growing life within her evident in each step. He knew she struggled with the secrets surrounding her husband's death and wondered how anyone could throw their life away for gambling—games on the Internet that meant nothing. If he'd had someone like Aubree, he would've treasured every moment and saved every penny for a home with a white picket fence.

Jason had assisted the FBI techs in running a search on every combination of phone number similar to Devin's cell phone. They were attempting to find the number the man tried to call that day. They highlighted any person of interest connected to these numbers, but the list was exhausting. Because the original call Aubree received was placed using a disposable cell phone, the trace didn't give them any more information.

Jason kept hoping they would get a break and find that one piece of evidence they needed to corner a suspect, but nothing surfaced. He leaned toward the window, wishing there was a way to shelter Aubree from the world.

Aubree looked up and waved at him. Jason felt his cheeks grow warm, and he waved back. On his way out of the house, he vowed to himself to keep her safe and hoped someday he would see a smile on her beautiful face again.

✳ ✳ ✳

Aubree dipped a toe in the cool water of the stream and thought about Jason. The worry lines in his forehead were constantly creased, and she knew he was doing his best to solve her case and keep her safe. The search for details seemed endless.

Everything was coming to a dead end, yet Aubree was still in protective custody—a point she'd argued many times with Jason. The last argument had taken place only yesterday.

"I don't understand how I could be a threat to anyone. I never saw the man who called," she said. "They killed the secretary of defense. That's what they wanted to do, right?"

Jason massaged his temples in the familiar pattern that showed his frustration. "Aubree, we haven't identified any type of connection between the shooter we apprehended aboard the *Midway* and Tidmore, who was killed the same day as your husband. We're working with the San Diego chief of police and questioning everyone on duty that day, but we don't have solid leads."

"I know, but I'm not helping the situation either. I've remembered everything there is to remember about that conversation. I don't know anything else."

He threw his hands in the air and pointed a finger at her. "The people who orchestrated Robert Walden's assassination don't know how much you heard or remember. Maybe that guy thought you heard more than you did, or maybe there's more to it all. I don't know, but I do know you're still a viable threat to them."

Aubree stiffened. "Okay, I believe you, but have you thought about my request?"

He shook his head.

"Please, Jason; I need my mother to be here with me when the baby comes."

"It would mean pulling a lot of strings, and it's not the wisest decision," Jason said.

"If I have to, I'll leave. You can't keep me here," Aubree insisted.

His face flushed with anger, and the intensity in his green eyes was commanding, but Aubree stood her ground. The muscles around his jaw clenched, and he said, "I'll get your mother here."

Back in the garden, Aubree smiled. She could stick it out a little longer knowing her mom would be there in ten days. She sat up as her uterus tightened. The false contractions were beginning to get very uncomfortable. Aubree attempted to focus on reading her romance novel, but she kept rereading the same lines as she tried to breathe through the contractions. Finally, she tossed the book aside and stood up, only to sit back down as another contraction came—this one harder than any of the others.

"Are you okay?" Garrett Sanderson walked through the French doors and knelt beside her.

"I'm having a lot of contractions."

"Do you think you're in labor?"

"I don't know," she said. Aubree noted the excitement in his voice. Sanderson had been pretty protective of her while she'd been there. His watch beeped again, and Aubree smiled. Every hour he stopped his work to check on her. He held out a tray with ice water and fruit.

"You don't have to wait on me," she protested.

"I want to make sure you're comfortable." She watched him reset his watch. "Jason said if I wasn't nice, you might jump ship."

Aubree blushed. "I'm sorry to be such a pain."

Sanderson laughed. "I don't mind."

He held out the same large hand that had intimidated her the first night she met him. "Do you want me to help you inside?"

"Yes, I'd like to walk around and see if that helps." She leaned against his hefty torso, and he helped her into the kitchen. He poured a glass of lemonade and watched her closely.

"Are you remembering to breathe?"

Aubree clutched her stomach. "I'm trying." She winced and headed for a soft chair in the living room.

"Let's go ahead and start timing those contractions." Sanderson motioned to his wristwatch. "I think they're the real thing this time."

"They feel a lot stronger." Aubree tried to push back the anxiety rising within her. If her baby came early, would Jason still be able to get her mom here?

After about thirty minutes of timing, Jason came through the security door with some supplies. When he saw Aubree and Sanderson, his eyes widened. "Why didn't you call me?"

"Because we were making sure these were the real thing," Sanderson answered and then smiled proudly. "And they are. This baby's coming!"

"Already?" Jason raked his fingers through his hair and stared at Aubree's stomach.

She nodded and tensed as her uterus contracted again. Unclenching her fists, she tried to remember the relaxation techniques she'd been studying. "They're about four minutes apart now."

"Four minutes! What are you waiting for, then?" Jason said.

"The nurse said the contractions need to last about a minute each and go on for an hour before we take Aubree in," Sanderson said.

"But aren't you in pain?" Jason crouched beside Aubree.

Her jaw clenched, and she sucked in a breath of air. "It's going to get a lot worse, I guess."

Jason stood. "I'll get your hospital bag for you."

As he hurried down the hallway, she smiled. Two trained FBI agents were worrying over her and neither of them had kids. "Can you start the transfer for my mother?" she asked Sanderson. She knew her mom would have to take two different flights and at least one bus ride to get in the vicinity indirectly in case she was followed.

"I'll make some calls," Jason said before Sanderson could answer. He set Aubree's hospital bag and the diaper bag she'd packed for the baby on the floor. As she continued to feel the strong sensations of the contractions coursing through her body, she thought about how much she and Devin had looked forward to this day. Although it was still painful to think of Devin, she missed her husband and wished he could be with her.

A few minutes later, Jason returned to the living room. Aubree managed to squeak out, "Did you talk to my mom?"

"I didn't contact her directly. I've set up a chain of contact to get things moving." He knelt beside her chair. "I think we should head for the hospital now."

She sucked in a breath and squeezed his hand. "All right, let's go then."

It didn't take long to get settled in the car, and Sanderson insisted on driving. The security measures to travel to the hospital were thorough. It was a private hospital, and the FBI was prepared for this unique circumstance with their witness, but Jason was uptight about her safety. He'd handpicked the agents who would be involved with the security detail at the hospital.

All of these thoughts swirled through her mind as they drove. She watched her hands and tried to keep them relaxed in an effort to stay focused on her breathing. The contractions continued to come. She squeezed her eyes shut and visualized Devin holding their newborn child. The image was always a bit blurry because she still didn't know if she was having a boy or a girl.

Aubree kept up her visualization and relaxation techniques through all of the hassle of getting into the hospital and being prepped for delivery. She looked away when they inserted the IV into her hand.

After the doctor checked her and found she was dilated to a five, Aubree kept an eye on the clock. It was already one-thirty in the afternoon, and she'd been in labor for roughly four hours. Two nurses were helping her, and two concerned FBI agents stood outside her door, but she still felt alone. Jason and Sanderson had offered to stay with her during the birth, but Aubree thought it might be awkward to have them there. So they waited in the hall.

Gasping through another strong contraction, she tried to compartmentalize her feelings and think about the joy soon to come. But it was harder to follow her mother's advice than she had expected. Moisture leaked from her eyes and ran down the sides of her face, but it took too much energy to cry. Aubree kept swallowing and repeating a silent prayer for peace in her heart.

TEN

* * *

J UST WHEN SHE THOUGHT she couldn't push anymore, Aubree heard
the nurse's excited cheers. "You did it! She's here."

She let her head fall back against the pillow in exhaustion. The
doctor held up her baby, and Aubree blinked away tears of joy. "It's a
girl."

When they placed the whimpering baby girl in her arms, Aubree
felt so much peace and love that she actually looked around her—half
expecting Devin to be standing right there.

She smiled at the tiny face looking up at her with bits of dark curls
all over her head. "Hello, Scarlett. I'm so excited you're here." Aubree
felt as if her heart might burst with love. She gently kissed Scarlett.
Caressing the soft skin of her baby brought a thrill to her heart, and she
cuddled the seven-pound, two-ounce bundle closer.

After Aubree was moved to a maternity room and settled in with
her baby, the nurse said, "There are two rough and tough FBI agents out
there dying to see this little girl."

"I guess we've kept them waiting long enough," Aubree said.

"That's what they've been saying. They know she was born at 6:25,
and they can't imagine what we're doing in here."

The clock on the wall ticked steadily. It was already 7:45 p.m., and the
hours of the day had been eaten up by painful contractions, but Aubree
felt relief now when she looked at her sweet baby. The nurse opened the
door a crack and whispered to Sanderson and Jason. Aubree smiled when
she heard them scrambling to get inside.

"That was worse than any stakeout I've ever been on," Sanderson said with a grin. "This guy was about to drive me crazy with all of his worrying."

Jason blushed and slugged him. "Don't let him fool you. He was just as concerned as I was."

"It's nice to know you guys are in my corner." Aubree tucked the blanket tighter around her wide-eyed baby. "Would you like to meet Scarlett?"

They stepped closer. "She's beautiful," Jason said. "Look at that dark hair."

"She's got curls, too, from her daddy." Aubree brushed her fingers softly against the brown tufts of hair. "Would you like to hold her?" She held Scarlett out for Jason, and his eyes softened.

"Are you sure?"

She handed the infant to him. "You better take your chance now before her grandma gets here."

"I'll have until tomorrow, then." Jason held the baby like she might break if he moved.

"Really? Thanks so much for doing that—for getting her here," Aubree said.

"Well, you didn't leave me much choice," Jason said.

After Sanderson took his turn holding Scarlett, the nurse ushered the two agents back out into the hallway. "She needs to feed the baby and get some rest."

Aubree stared into Scarlett's eyes and hummed softly to her. Even though it hadn't turned out like her original plans, she was a mother now, and nothing else mattered.

It was nearly four in the morning when Aubree heard someone in her room. Her eyelids felt heavy with fatigue, and she struggled to focus on the figure approaching her bed. The nurse checked Aubree's IV bag; the fluid was nearly gone.

"Have you come to take out my IV?" Aubree asked.

"Oh! You're awake. I'm sorry, I didn't want to wake you—I guess it's hard to sleep when you're in pain though, huh?" The nurse stepped closer to her. "Let me check your vitals."

Aubree closed her eyes while the nurse checked her vitals and wished she could just go back to sleep.

"Having a baby is like being run over by a truck," the nurse said and chuckled.

Aubree nodded and then watched the nurse take out a needle.

"This pain medicine will help you feel better."

"No, I'm okay. I took a pain pill earlier," Aubree said.

The nurse fiddled with the tube connected to Aubree's IV. "This is just to last you through the night."

"No. When I take too much pain medicine, it makes me sick."

The nurse didn't hesitate when Aubree protested, and Aubree felt her heart rate increase as she watched the needle approaching the IV bag.

"Oh, this won't do that," the nurse said.

Aubree realized that maybe this nurse wasn't here to help her feel better. She pulled herself to a sitting position. "Jason!" Aubree cried. "Help me!"

The nurse jumped back in alarm as the door burst open, and Jason and Sanderson ran in. Lights flooded the room. "What are you doing?" Jason demanded, grabbing the nurse's arm.

"I'm giving her some morphine like the doctor ordered." Her voice trembled.

"Morphine! She's allergic to morphine," Jason shouted.

Aubree felt like she was in a bad dream. She watched Sanderson grab the syringe from the nurse and examine it.

"Where's her chart? I want to see the orders," Sanderson demanded.

"It's on the computer. The doctor ordered it up because her pain level was a seven," the nurse said.

"I was sleeping. I never asked for more pain meds," Aubree said. She grabbed the bed sheets, wiped her sweaty palms, and took a few shallow breaths.

Jason tugged on the nurse's arm, leading her toward the laptop hooked to the hospital's mainframe. "Show me."

Sanderson bent over Aubree's bed. "Are you okay?"

She nodded, and another nurse wearing pink scrubs entered the room, pushing the newborn cart. Aubree leaned forward when she heard Scarlett's cries. The nurse looked around and frowned. "Is everything okay here?"

"No," Jason answered and pointed to the other nurse. "She was about to give Aubree a lethal dose of morphine."

The nurse wiped her eyes. "I promise I didn't know she was allergic. I was just following orders."

Jason typed rapidly on the laptop. "Someone's tampered with her medical chart." He pulled out his cell phone and pushed a few buttons. "Agent Edwards here, we need tech control at the hospital on the Stewart case now." He paused and shook his head. "Either someone's hacked into the system or entered it from the premises."

Scarlett's cries escalated, and Aubree's heart pounded as she listened to several different conversations. The nurse in pink told Sanderson that Aubree needed to feed the baby, the other nurse kept apologizing between sobs, and Jason finished his phone call with an expletive and clenched his fist. He looked at Sanderson. "We're out of here."

"Get the doctor up here—Aubree's checking out," Sanderson barked at the nurse in pink scrubs. He glared at the other nurse. "Come with me. I need a statement from you."

"Give me my baby." Aubree's voice rose above the commotion, and Jason stepped toward the bassinet. He lifted Scarlett carefully and handed her to Aubree.

"Go ahead and feed Scarlett, and then we'll leave as soon as the doctor gets here."

The tension in the room had charged Aubree's nerves until her hands shook, but she held Scarlett and took a deep breath. Jason pulled a curtain around Aubree's bed, and she tried to quiet her screaming infant.

The nurse in pink scrubs helped calm Scarlett by rubbing her feet. "It's okay now," she said. "I'll help you. Don't cry." She seemed to speak to both mother and baby. Aubree listened to the soothing note of her voice and focused on feeding Scarlett.

By the time Aubree finished nursing Scarlett, the hospital was in a state of high alert, with FBI officials swarming the nurse's stations and checking every computer port. They left the hospital in a rush as Aubree's body protested every movement.

When they pushed her out in a wheelchair, Aubree noticed Sanderson's brow creased with tension. Scarlett slept peacefully in her car seat, and Aubree continually pushed down the hysteria that threatened to bubble over at any minute. They took an indirect route to return to the house, with Jason worrying constantly about getting there safely.

When the house had passed a full sweep, and Scarlett was tucked into her bassinet, Aubree curled up on her bed and stared into the darkness. She was too exhausted to cry, but the raw fear coursing through her body kept her awake. Focusing on thoughts of her mother's arrival the next morning finally helped ease her to sleep.

✳ ✳ ✳

Madeline arrived just after eleven that morning and couldn't take her eyes off her new granddaughter. She rocked the infant and nuzzled her soft skin. "She is absolutely gorgeous!" she exclaimed for the hundredth time. "Aubree, I think she has your mouth. Look at those rosebud lips."

Scarlett slept with a peaceful smile in her grandmother's arms. Aubree watched her and hoped her own smile would be peaceful again someday. After she told her mom about the incident at the hospital, Jason felt the wrath of Madeline's fiery temper.

"After all she's been through, you couldn't even keep her safe while she was having her baby? You promised me."

He pursed his lips and shook his head. "I know. I'm sorry, but Aubree and the baby will be safe now."

"How can I be sure of that?" Madeline asked.

Jason frowned. "Part of the reason I agreed to let you come visit is because I knew Aubree would be leaving the area soon."

"What?" Aubree's eyes immediately began to water.

"Oh dear," Madeline said. "I knew it was coming, but I kept hoping."

Jason licked his lips. "I know. We were all hoping, but with this happening and the other activity going on with your case, headquarters have heightened security again."

Aubree wiped at her eyes with the baby's burp rag. "What other activity?"

"I'm not sure. All I know now is you will soon move to a more permanent protective location."

"When will I have to leave?" Aubree passed the baby to Madeline with shaking hands.

"I'm going in tomorrow to be briefed on more details." He smiled as he looked at Madeline holding her tiny grandbaby and then stepped closer to Aubree. "I know you're upset, but this will be the only real chance you'll have at a normal life for now. You'll be able to take Scarlett for walks without looking over your shoulder."

Aubree clasped her hands together. Would she ever stop looking over her shoulder or hearing that gruff voice echo through her mind? She shook her head and resolved to concentrate on her mom and Scarlett—to savor every moment they had together.

* * *

The information Jason brought back from his briefing the next day wasn't good. He asked Aubree to sit in the office adjoining the kitchen of the home. Madeline rocked Scarlett in the next room because she wasn't allowed to hear the report. Sanderson paced by the computer and waited for Jason to speak.

"Our tech guys found the source of the entry. One of the computers in the nurse's station was left unattended for three minutes, and that's all it took." Jason rubbed his eyes and continued. "Whoever entered that information was only a few yards from your room."

Aubree gasped and covered her mouth.

Jason cleared his throat. "That's not all. The FBI finally traced a connection between Tidmore and the man who killed Secretary Walden. A known illegal arms dealer is linked to both of them." Jason paced the room in frustration. "He's big-time, Aubree. He has a lot backing him and possibly more fire power than the FBI."

"So what? If he's that powerful, why would he be looking for me?" Aubree folded her arms and scowled.

"He knows who you are, and someone *is* looking for you," Jason said. Then he glanced at Agent Sanderson.

"What? What aren't you telling me?" Aubree asked Sanderson directly.

"Your picture's been passed around in some of our monitored circles. Someone's looking for you." Sanderson sighed and wrinkled his brow. "We don't know why. We only know they want to find you."

Aubree sat back in her chair and looked at her hands. They were puffy and bruised from the IV. There hadn't even been time for her to heal from giving birth yet. She wished she didn't have to think about any of this.

She didn't want to believe what they were telling her—that her life was still in danger. Her skin prickled with fear. "How could they even get a picture of me?"

Sanderson shook his head. "I wish we knew how these criminals managed to do half the things they do."

Jason stood still and rubbed a hand along the back of his neck. "I feel like we're still missing something. It seems like Aubree can't possibly know anything to threaten these guys, but they think she does."

"It's okay. I'll do it. I'll go wherever you tell me—whatever I need to do to keep Scarlett safe." Aubree spoke quietly, but with a firm resolve. It was time she quit fighting against those who were trying to protect her.

"I'm sorry. I know it's not fair, but it's the only kind of life we can offer you." Jason folded his arms, and Aubree watched his fiery tattoo move with the twitch of his muscles. She bowed her head and angrily wiped her eyes.

"It's going to be a few weeks. You need time to recover, and we need time to get everything set up," Jason said.

Sanderson stood and offered her his hand. "Now go take care of that baby, and try not to worry."

Aubree stepped onto the cold tile of the kitchen and heard the office door shut behind her. She shuffled to her room and collapsed on the bed. It took some time for her to calm down enough to tell her mom she was entering protective custody permanently.

Madeline cried with her and then blew her nose and said, "That'll have to be enough crying. We're not going to worry about your uncertain future right now. We'll enjoy Scarlett and the time we have together." She rubbed Aubree's back and stroked her hair. "And when it comes time, you're going to take hold of that life they're offering you—no matter how upside-down and turned around it may seem—and live it."

ELEVEN

Jason popped the back off the cell phone and slid the battery out. He flipped over the tiny transmitter and inserted it in the phone, and then he replaced the battery. Working quickly, he programmed a few numbers into the phone and nodded. He would be able to track every phone call and text message from this phone without looking into the FBI's mainframe. He hoped it would be enough.

"Mom, it's coming too fast. I'm afraid to be alone." Aubree folded a brand-new pink sleeper and put it in a box. She was packing clothing to be shipped to their new destination. Four-week-old Scarlett slept in her bassinet, ignoring the bustle of activity surrounding the preparation for their departure.

Madeline tucked some of her clothing in a suitcase. "I keep praying they'll find whoever did this and put them in jail so you can stay," she said. "But I know this won't last forever."

They continued to pack their belongings in silence. Scarlett's soft breathing blended with the rustle of clothing. Madeline would leave in the morning, and Aubree knew she would be next. Glancing at the freckles on her arms, she wondered if she would ever return to California. Her life as she had known it—the life she was supposed to be living with Devin and their child—didn't exist anymore.

"I'll wait this out a few more months, Mom. If they haven't found any more evidence on my case by then, I'll come see you."

"Promise me you'll be careful and do what they say." Madeline zipped her suitcase shut. "I trust them, and if they say you're in danger, I'd rather not see you if it means you'll stay safe."

Aubree continued folding clothing. "I'll try, Mom. Did you get a security system installed?"

"Yes, Jason suggested I go with Platinum, and they set it up right after Devin's funeral. You don't need to worry about me. I've got round-the-clock surveillance, and Jason said the FBI is keeping tabs on me." She held out a spiral-bound notebook. "I made this for you."

The brown cover was decorated with pink polka dots, and Aubree could tell the pages had all been written on. "You made me another notebook?" Aubree took it and held it to her chest. "Thank you."

"I hope it'll remind you that although life is difficult, it moves in stages." Madeline hugged Aubree. "This stage you're in is terribly hard, but I believe it will pass on to better things."

After a painful good-bye the following morning, Madeline left on what she called her "wild goose chase" to get back home. Aubree didn't know her mother's travel plans, but Jason said Madeline wouldn't be home for two days.

Later that evening, Aubree watched the minute hand crawl through the hour. Madeline's FBI transport was scheduled to check in with Jason at eight o'clock. At 8:15 p.m., Aubree clenched the sofa pillow as Jason paced the room, hitting redial.

They both jumped when his phone rang. "You're late." He frowned, put a hand on the back of his head, and closed his eyes. He walked through the kitchen and into the office.

Aubree sucked in a breath and slid to the edge of the couch, listening to the murmur of Jason's voice. She straightened her shoulders and stood before tiptoeing through the kitchen and leaning against the outside wall of the office. She heard Jason push a button, and the speakerphone clicked on. Her heart pounded, and she held her breath. She heard the other agent talking.

"We were being tracked. We went silent so that they wouldn't pick up any signals."

Jason cursed. "When did you lose them?"

"About thirty-five minutes ago."

"What evidence did you collect?" Jason asked. Aubree heard him opening drawers. Papers shuffled, and she heard the click of a pen as he began taking notes.

"Three males, wired and armed."

Aubree gasped, and Jason poked his head out of the office. He raised his eyebrows at her and punched another button on the phone to resume the conversation in private. She was too angry to care that she'd been caught eavesdropping. Folding her arms, she stepped into the open door-way of the office and glared at Jason.

He didn't seem surprised that Madeline had been followed. She watched with a sick feeling in her stomach as he scribbled notes. Had he used Madeline as bait? She felt the heat of anger coursing through her veins, and when Jason ended the call she narrowed her eyes.

"Why were you listening in on my conversation?"

Aubree ignored his question. "What did you do?"

Jason took a step back. "Whoa! Your mom is okay, and we may have a lead on whoever was tracking them."

"Did you use my mother as bait?"

"What? No! Why would you think that?" Jason held up his hands.

She folded her arms and stared at him for a second before answering. "Because you don't seem surprised that she was followed."

Jason clasped his hands behind his head and looked at the ceiling. "Of course I'm not surprised. I've known for a while now that someone might have been leaking information. I put a note out in the witness protection department that *you* were leaving today, not your mom."

Aubree leaned back against the wall, bewildered.

"We're getting closer to isolating the transfer of information, but I can't tell if this information is moving on your case only or on all new placements in the witness protection program."

She was quiet for a moment. "They're going to kill me, aren't they?" She lifted her head slowly and met Jason's gaze.

Jason's eyes flickered, and he hesitated, "No, they're not going to hurt you." He took a deep breath. "I shouldn't have told you anything. I would never put you or your mother in danger. She'll be home tomor-row. There's a lot more to these investigations than you would ever understand."

"I understand, Jason, but I'll never get my life back, and I hope you don't think I'm ungrateful because I'm worried about my family." She walked down the hall. "I just hope you know what you're doing." She closed the door to her room.

✳ ✳ ✳

In January, Aubree was given a file of papers on her new location, identity, and other kinds of information pertinent to her protective custody. She took her mother's advice. She kept her chin up through all of the planning and briefing on her new life. She tried not to think about the doubts she had and the difficulties with the investigation. Jason kept her busy, quizzing her on small details.

"What's your name?" he asked for the thousandth time as he paced around the backyard garden.

"Jolynn Dobson," Aubree answered automatically.

"Where do you live?"

"Omaha, Nebraska." She cuddled Scarlett and shaded her eyes from the sunlight.

"Where are you from?"

"Oh, around—how about you?"

"Good, Aubree. That's what I want you to keep practicing. Deflect the personal questions and become a great listener to other people's information." Jason sat in the deck chair next to her and smiled at Scarlett. "She's a cute baby. Where's her daddy?"

"He's missing her right now, that's for sure. Good thing we have digital cameras these days. He's in Europe on business."

"Really? Where in Europe?"

Aubree didn't miss a beat. "Pretty much anywhere he can sell his new software program. What does your wife do?"

Jason clapped his hands. "You're really getting the hang of this."

"Yeah, well, let's hope I don't have to use my skills too much," Aubree said. "I'd rather keep to myself."

"You're lucky you have Scarlett for that." Jason twirled a small blue flower in front of the baby. "You'll have your hands full caring for her, and what better excuse do you need?"

"Hey, you guys ready for some grub?" Sanderson poked his head out the door. "Aubree, maybe you can practice with me while we eat."

"Looks like I'm going to have to get really good with excuses." Aubree sighed, and both the FBI agents chuckled.

After being quizzed during lunch, Aubree retreated to her bedroom to feed Scarlett and rest. She rocked the infant in her arms, amazed at how much she'd already grown. In a couple weeks, it would be time for her two-month check-up, and Scarlett already weighed twelve pounds, with fat rolls appearing on her arms and legs.

She kissed Scarlett's dark curls and thought about the new life being built for her in Omaha. A stay-at-home mom married to a software guru. She would try to blend into a small, two-bedroom home in the quiet neighborhood the FBI had selected for her.

The witness protection program would cover her expenses for now, so all she had to do was concentrate on staying undercover and alive. Aubree shivered as she thought about the self-defense skills Sanderson was teaching her. This definitely wasn't the way she'd planned to spend her time as a new mother. The FBI allowed her time to recover and prepare for the move, but the house was on close watch.

Aubree wrote a letter to her mother but couldn't give any details about where she was headed. It was hard to believe she was going halfway across the country to a state she'd never visited before. Jason told her it wasn't as if they'd just drawn the name of the state out of a hat. A lot of planning went into the assignment. Jason would still be her case officer during her time in Nebraska, and few people would be privy to the information concerning Aubree's whereabouts.

"Are you ready to go?" Sanderson knocked on the open bedroom door.

"I think so." She picked up Scarlett and the diaper bag.

"I'll load these in the car, and we'll be on our way." Sanderson smiled at her as he hefted her luggage.

Aubree followed slowly and stopped to glance in the mirror. Within the hour, her appearance would change significantly. She fingered her shoulder length, strawberry blonde hair and chewed on the inside of her cheek. Jason said it would be a drastic change, and she had never been a daredevil when it came to her hair. She looked in the mirror again and shrugged. "Guess there's a first time for everything," she told her reflection.

Unfortunately, Jason hadn't minced words when he said drastic. A couple hours later, in a small salon in an FBI office, a government image specialist twirled the chair around to face a large mirror. Aubree gasped.

She had watched as long pieces of her hair fell to the ground, but she wasn't quite prepared for what she saw.

A raven-haired woman looked back from the mirror. Her hair was short, and it framed her chin line. Aubree reached up and touched the back of her hair, which rose in an A-line style. Her neck was bare, and her eyebrows, which had always been blonde and non-descript, now accented her face in a dark brown color. She turned her head from side to side and noticed reddish highlights streaking through her black hair.

"What do you think?" the hairdresser asked.

"Wow ... I guess." Aubree pasted on a smile. "I don't recognize myself. Thanks for your help."

"I know it'll take some getting used to, but pretty soon you won't freak out every time you look in the mirror." The woman smiled and winked at her.

Aubree laughed. "I hope so."

"I'll go tell them you're ready." The woman exited the room.

A minute later, Aubree heard the handle turning and looked up, expecting to see Jason. Instead, a tall brunette walked into the room.

"Hi, Miranda." Aubree hadn't seen the agent since she'd been re-assigned a few months ago. Aubree knew Jason didn't like her, but she'd never had any problems with Agent Olsen.

"Wow! Is that really Aubree Stewart in there?" Miranda walked around the chair and stared at Aubree. "It looks nice."

"Do you really think so?"

"Yes. Now smile as if you like it too, and let me take a picture of you for your file." Miranda held up a small digital camera.

"I thought this wasn't going in my file," Aubree said.

"Because they don't keep many pictures of people in the witness protection program?" Miranda said and winked.

Aubree shrugged. "Something like that."

"Everybody has a file on everything. Some of the info is just hidden deeper." Miranda clicked the camera. "The inside of the file folder will probably be the only thing to ever see this picture." She pushed the button on the camera again. "Now you take care of yourself and have some fun, okay?"

"I'll try." Aubree ran her hand through her hair and smiled.

"Sorry to shoot and run, but they like to keep me busy around here." Miranda waved and opened the door.

"Good-bye," Aubree said. She wondered if she'd ever see Miranda again or any of the other people who had helped her lately. She doubted it.

Scarlett fussed, and Aubree realized it was time to feed her again. In a few hours, she'd be saying good-bye to California and taking an indirect route to Omaha. While she fed Scarlett, she thought about the changes taking place in her life. The room was quiet, and the light overhead illuminated everything with a false brightness. Aubree listened to the hum of the heating vent and cuddled Scarlett. Glancing in the mirror again, she wondered if the old Aubree would be lost forever. Would Jolynn Dobson overtake the fading memories she held of Devin before he died?

A staccato knock announced Jason's entrance to the room, and Aubree quickly wiped the pained expression from her face. Jason was surprised at Aubree's new look. He lifted his chin and smiled. "That's what I'm talking about. You're going to do fine."

He quizzed her again as they drove toward the airport and reassured her that everything was in order. "I don't want you to worry," he said. "When you're nervous, you make mistakes."

"I know," Aubree answered. She looked through her new purse and the unfamiliar ID cards with Jolynn Dobson's name all over them. She took a deep breath and pushed the desperate feelings of anxiety away. "I'm ready to do this."

Jason shook her hand at the airport. "Now, remember. We have you flying under the name Kelsey Riker on the first flight. Do not use the name Jolynn Dobson until you are on the second flight into Nebraska."

"I hope no one asks me my name," Aubree said.

Jason smiled. "They probably won't. Here's where I hand you off, but don't worry, there's an FBI agent flying with you."

"But I thought no one is supposed to know who I am."

"He doesn't. He thinks you're someone connected to an entirely different case. He's supposed to be alert for any kind of suspicious behavior and be ready to protect you and Scarlett."

Her eyes stung, and she put a hand over her trembling lips. Scarlett cooed from her car seat, and Aubree swung it back and forth, blinking back tears.

"There will be someone to pick you up at the airport in Omaha. They'll be holding a sign that says ITEC Convention," Jason whispered.

"Just walk up to him and say, 'Do I have time to use the restroom before we go?' and he'll deliver you to the next point."

"Okay." Her mind buzzed with all of the information. Jason had warned her the previous week that there would be last minute details she'd have to remember about her arrival in Nebraska. She tried to calm her mind and repeat the information he'd just given her. "Are you sure this is safe?"

Jason's jaw tensed, and his eyes narrowed. "I thought you trusted me."

"I do, but I'm scared."

He pulled her to his chest. "It's my job to keep you safe, Aubree, but this is more than a job to me."

The clean scent of his aftershave lingered in the air, and Aubree relaxed into his arms. Jason held her for a moment, then backed away and cleared his throat. His eyes looked moist, and he grasped her hand and squeezed it. Aubree hesitated, unsure of what to say or do next. Jason blushed and released her hand. He reached into his suit pocket.

"Remember who you are." He handed her a silver cell phone. "I want you to call me on speed dial three when you've made contact at the airport. Then throw this phone away. There's another in your purse, and I'll tell you what to do with that when you call."

"Thanks for everything, Jason." Aubree slipped the phone into her purse and checked to make sure she had everything she needed.

"No problem. Thanks for doing this." He smiled at her and Scarlett. "Keep your chin up. We're going to get to the bottom of this."

"I'm counting on it," Aubree said. She smiled at him and walked away, humming a lullaby to Scarlett to keep her mind occupied. She didn't want to think about trusting Jason with her frightening future or about the fact that the FBI still didn't know who she was running from.

TWELVE

* * *

THE FLIGHT TO DENVER, Colorado, was uneventful. Aubree studied all of the passengers for anything out of the ordinary. When she noticed how tightly she gripped the arm rests, she recalled the relaxation techniques she'd been taught and plastered a smile on her face. Scarlett was very cooperative on the airplane, sleeping most of the way, and Aubree held her breath, praying she would stay asleep.

It would have been nice to take a direct flight to Omaha, but changing things up a bit would make it harder for her to be followed. The airport in Denver was crowded. Aubree clutched Scarlett with a firm grasp and hurried to her boarding area. The agent sent to tail her hadn't introduced himself, but Aubree felt like she was being watched.

As she walked around a wide pillar, a man bumped into her, sending her off-balance. She cried out as another man ripped her carry-on bag from her shoulder and took off running. As she fell toward the hard ground, Aubree curled around Scarlett and screamed. Just before impact, she felt someone behind her, breaking her fall.

"Stay right where you are. I'll be back." The man who'd caught her disentangled himself and ran down the corridor of the airport.

Aubree remained in a heap on the floor, terrified of what this meant. People stopped and stared, and although only seconds passed, Aubree felt like she was on a stage, with everyone looking at her. The blood pounded in her head. Had they found her already? Did the man steal her bag as some sort of signal so she could be eliminated? Scarlett wailed, and Aubree held her close with shaking arms.

"Miss, can I help you?" An airport security officer held out his hand. Aubree took it and allowed him to lift her to her feet.

"That man stole my bag," she stammered.

"He didn't get far. One of the other commuters knocked him down." He began writing on a clipboard. "Let's get a report filed for you. What's your name?"

"My name—I—" Aubree stared at him. His pen was poised ready to write, but she couldn't remember her cover name.

"That won't be necessary. She's not pressing charges." The man who broke Aubree's fall ran toward them. His face was red, and he breathed heavily, but he held her carry-on.

"What—" Aubree started as the man pulled out a badge.

"Agent Stokes, FBI, and I'll be filing those charges."

The security officer lifted his eyebrows and smiled. "Good then. Guess I'm done here."

"Thank you. Your perp is handcuffed, and security detail will transport him," Agent Stokes said. He turned to Aubree. "Are you okay?"

She shook her head and felt the tremors of fear running through her body.

"Now, don't fall apart on me. It was just some idiot thief." He smiled and two dimples appeared on his cheeks. "Come over here and sit down." He directed Aubree to a waiting area and sat beside her.

It seemed like she was a blinking target for trouble, and her knees were trembling with the effort to stay calm. Scarlett stopped crying, and Aubree took some deep breaths. "What if he wasn't just a thief?" She gazed around the terminal. The minor interruption was over, and everyone moved swiftly through the corridor again. "Why did you leave me?"

Stokes leaned toward her and whispered. "I'm sorry, but I knew you weren't alone. There's a ghost on the lookout for you—I knew you were covered."

"You mean there are two of you?"

"Yeah, but we didn't want you drawing too much attention to yourself by trying to find out who we were." He winked at her. "Are you going to be okay?"

Aubree nodded. She felt someone watching her and lifted her head. It was a woman. Her dark brown hair was pulled back in a ponytail, and she stood by the escalators. Aubree watched her go up the escalator, but the woman didn't look back. Maybe it had been her imagination, but she thought the woman had averted her eyes just as Aubree had looked up. Something seemed familiar about her. Aubree chewed on her bottom lip and squinted, but the woman was gone.

"Let me help you get on your next flight. We'll be taking some extra precautions in case we've been compromised." Agent Stokes lifted her carry-on and walked beside her through the terminal.

Aubree tried to resist looking over her shoulder—she still had a feeling she was being watched. Then she remembered the other agent following them and told herself to stay calm.

When her plane touched down in Omaha, the anxiety in her stomach felt like boiling acid. Agent Stokes stayed in her peripheral vision as she walked briskly to the baggage claim. There was a man holding a sign just as Jason had said there would be. Aubree walked toward the bright blue ITEC letters on the sign and smiled. "Do I have time to use the restroom before we go?" she asked, trying to keep her voice from squeaking.

"Yes, ma'am," he replied in a southern drawl. "Let me help you with your bags first."

Aubree pointed out her suitcase and handed him her carry-on, and he pointed to the restroom. She kept repeating *act normal*, and *stay calm* in her head. She called Jason when she was in the bathroom stall.

"You made it." He answered on the first ring. "I talked to Agent Stokes. How are you holding up?"

"Good," Aubree whispered. "Now what?"

"You're going to ride with your contact to a hotel, switch cars, and then you'll be driven to your new home. There will be two other agents tailing you the whole way, and your home is under surveillance. Remember to throw this cell phone away and call me on speed dial three from the other phone when you get to your house."

"Okay. I'll talk to you soon, I guess."

"You're doing great. You're almost there," Jason said.

Aubree shut the phone off, popped the battery out, and, after washing her hands, wrapped it in some paper towels and threw it in the garbage can. She carried Scarlett back into the noisy airport and followed her driver outside.

Everything happened exactly according to plan, and Aubree relaxed a bit after they switched cars and headed out of the city. By the time they reached her new neighborhood, Scarlett was hungry again, and so was Aubree. The driver pulled into a single driveway surrounded by leafless, tangled rosebushes covered in frost. He handed Aubree a bag that contained a set of keys and a garage door opener.

The high pitches of the roof reminded Aubree of a quaint English cottage. The house was painted Wedgwood blue with white shutters around the front windows and window boxes underneath.

She walked tentatively up the front steps and pushed the key into the lock. It clicked, and she opened the door slowly. Stepping inside the entryway, she appraised the sitting room. It had large windows. The furniture didn't look brand new, but it exuded a comfortable air. She bounced Scarlett lightly as she walked into the kitchen. It opened up to a cozy breakfast nook that overlooked a back yard covered in snow.

"There's a lot of snow here for February," Aubree said to the driver, who was carrying her suitcases.

He nodded. "Yep. It'll be here for another month at least."

Aubree stifled a groan. "Thanks for bringing those in."

"There are more boxes in the garage. Would you like me to bring a few of them in?" He motioned to a door off the kitchen that led to the garage.

"That would be nice, thanks." Aubree followed him and peeked at the neat stack of boxes waiting to be unpacked. They were filled with clothes she had ordered for herself and Scarlett and a few other belongings. It was all new. There was nothing connected to the memory of her old life. The boxes were piled in front of a green SUV that Devin would've gone nuts over. Aubree knew the FBI had provided this vehicle with four-wheel drive in case she had to travel in the snow. It was ironic she would be driving the type of vehicle Devin had always dreamed of.

She turned around and walked back through the kitchen to the short hallway leading to a bathroom and two bedrooms. The rooms weren't overly large, but they seemed comfortable. A crib was set up in Scarlett's room along with a changing table and a rocking recliner. Aubree was grateful that so much thought had been given to her welfare.

"I think that's about all of the boxes, ma'am." The driver indicated the neat pile he had carried into the house. "Can I do anything else for you?"

"No, thank you so much."

"All right, then. Enjoy." He waved at her and let himself out the front door.

Aubree locked the door and carried Scarlett, who was wailing now, into the nursery. After checking her diaper, Aubree sat in the recliner and fed her baby. Scarlett immediately calmed down and gulped noisily. Aubree rocked for a few minutes and then pulled out the second cell phone. Once again, Jason picked up on the first ring.

"You're in place?"

"Yes. It's very nice. Thank you."

"I'm glad you like it. You may be there longer than we originally hoped."

"What?" Aubree sat up suddenly, and Scarlett whimpered in protest.

"We're getting closer with the information we have," Jason said, "but I got another report of someone looking for you. Someone who isn't connected to our arms dealer."

"But what does that mean?"

"It could mean that we've been barking up the wrong tree altogether, or it could just be a deliberate ploy to get us off his back. I don't know, and I can't share all the details," Jason said. "I'm sorry. I know it's not what you'd like to hear, but I wanted to tell you so—"

"—So I'd be grateful I'm living in the witness protection program?" Aubree sighed.

Jason chuckled. "Yeah, I know. Wishful thinking." He cleared his throat. "The fridge and pantry are stocked. All of your utilities are set up on an automatic payment plan. You shouldn't have to worry about anything for now."

"What about keeping in touch with my mother?" Aubree asked. "How will I know she's safe?"

"She's safe. There hasn't been any other suspicious activity. We'll work something out. You may be able to send letters through our agency. I'm not sure, but I'll be calling you on this cell phone every three weeks with an update on your case. If you need me or have questions, hit speed dial number three anytime."

"Okay, I will."

"Remember to follow protocol. Okay, Jolynn?"

Aubree hesitated only a split second before answering. "Yes. That's Mrs. Dobson to you."

"I'll talk to you in a few weeks," Jason said, and Aubree could hear a smile in his voice.

She closed the phone and murmured, "I don't know who I am anymore, Scarlett, but I'm so glad I have you."

Scarlett nuzzled into Aubree's chest, and within a few minutes, they had both dozed off. Aubree dreamed about Devin. They were walking together down the streets of San Diego pushing a stroller with a dark-haired baby. Then she heard a gruff voice calling her name. She turned and saw a horrible man chasing her. He was screaming something about a body.

She woke up in a sweat. Her eyes darted frantically around the darkened room. Then she remembered she was in Nebraska under the protection of the FBI. Only, it seemed she could go halfway around the world and still not escape the voice that had taken Devin from her and stripped away her identity. She held Scarlett and sighed. Would she ever feel safe again?

THIRTEEN

✳ ✳ ✳

I T WASN'T SUPPOSED TO be this long," Aubree snapped. "You told me I'd be here for two or three months—it's been five." She gripped her cell phone and stared out the front room window. The roses flourished in the late-June heat.

"I know. But it's more complicated than I could ever have imagined." Jason's voice was even and restrained. "It's not everyday the secretary of defense gets assassinated."

"But can't I stay with my mom? You could set up surveillance there."

"Aubree, every time I turn around, I've got one of my cover agents telling me about some new piece of scum looking for you. They know you have a baby; they know stuff about you I didn't even know. We think they've got your mom under surveillance."

Aubree exhaled slowly. "Is my mom safe?"

"Yes, but I'm sorry. You won't be able to talk to her for awhile. We're doing the best we can."

Aubree didn't say anything. She thought about how every three weeks, Jason called her to see how she was doing. Twice he'd given her a number to call her mom, and Madeline had driven to a secure location for the phone call and waited for Aubree to contact her. Talking to her was really the only thing she had to look forward to. She even kept notes between their chats of the things Scarlett did so she would remember to report every detail. She swallowed and spoke into the phone again, "Thanks, Jason."

He cleared his throat, and she anticipated the next question with a clenched jaw.

"Are you still having nightmares?"

"Sometimes."

"I still think there's something we've missed in all of this. Maybe we should try hypnosis again."

"I've tried to be cooperative. I was hypnotized when I first moved out here, and I don't think it'll do any good to try again." She pushed a hand through her black hair. "I think I've recalled all the details of the conversation that matter."

"I know. It doesn't add up, though, and we've had the entire administration breathing down our necks. People don't kill the secretary of defense and get away with it. It's more than just a chance you'll recognize a voice. Someone thinks you know something that can hurt them. When I feel like you're safe, you'll be on the first flight home."

"Okay." She hung her head and whispered good-bye before ending the call.

The familiar stillness settled in the house with no one to talk to except Scarlett. Aubree tried to push down the lonely feeling rising from the pit of her stomach. At first the neighbors had come around to introduce themselves, but when Jolynn Dobson had acted standoffish, they hadn't tried to pursue a friendship. That was exactly how Aubree wanted it, and she filled her days with caring for Scarlett and watching her grow and change week by week. She'd developed a schedule of safe activities that she and Scarlett could do, one of which included cleaning the house. Even with a schedule, it was hard to fight the loneliness.

She walked toward the sounds of Scarlett playing in the family room. She didn't ever feel completely secure, but at times like these when Scarlett played quietly with a toy, she could almost forget the strangeness of her circumstances.

"How's my sweet little girl?" she said and tickled Scarlett's feet. It was hard to believe Scarlett was already eight months old and crawling after baby toys. Her hair wasn't quite as dark as it was at birth, but it still held plenty of ringlets. Her eyes had turned to a beautiful crystal blue, and with Aubree's hair still dyed dark most people commented that Scarlett was her spitting image. But when Aubree looked at her, all she could see was Devin.

Although the ache was still there, time had dulled the sharpness of her pain. Scarlett babbled and shook a flower-shaped rattle. The TV was on, but Aubree wasn't concentrating on it. She flipped through her cookbook; there was a new chicken casserole she wanted to try for supper tonight. Maybe she could mash some up to feed Scarlett.

The news anchor was reporting on the economic progress the state of Nebraska was making. "We're taking great strides in agriculture thanks to the new ethanol programs. The governor has been involved in the new green legislation since before he was elected. Now we'll go live to the corn belt's number one supporter, Governor Ferrin," the news anchor said.

When someone else began speaking, Aubree heard a voice that sent chills down her arms. It was like she was in a dream. The room began to spin, and she squinted at the TV, taking several ragged breaths. A man was speaking to a group of people.

"The state of Nebraska has a green future. Our corn belt and the new ethanol plants will breathe life into our economy and help struggling farmers."

It was hard for Aubree to focus on the man's face as her body shivered with the memory of the voice on Devin's cell phone. She closed her eyes and tried to clear her mind so she could compare the voice of her memory to the one she was hearing now on TV.

"With the endorsement of the federal government, the new green program will bolster our state with increased tax revenue and income for the working class. I think green is my new favorite color."

Her eyes snapped open. The speaker had chuckled, and it had been the same gruff cackle she remembered, but then she saw the identifying text line below the speaker. She shook her head to try to keep from remembering, but the conversation came anyway. "*Tidmore did the job, and the body is hidden in the manhole . . .*"

"No!" Aubree said. Scarlett jumped and dropped her toy with a whimper. Aubree bent down and scooped the baby into her arms. She closed her eyes again, but the voice was still there. She cradled Scarlett for a moment until the baby started reaching for her toy. Then Aubree arranged the blanket and sat her in front of the TV.

The governor of Nebraska ended his speech to a smattering of applause. Governor Brent Ferrin had the same speaking voice that had penetrated Aubree's worst nightmares for almost a year now. She reached for her cell phone and dialed Jason.

When he answered, Aubree's throat was so tight with tension that she could barely speak. "This is Jolynn. I need to speak with Jaybird." She said the code words that meant he needed to get to a private area to speak with her ASAP.

"I'm at the office, so we're good. What's up?" Jason said.

Aubree pinched the bridge of her nose and struggled to think how she could explain the thoughts racing through her mind. "I heard the voice. The one from the cell phone. It was Governor Ferrin, the governor of Nebraska." The words came in a rush, and she wasn't even sure how clearly she spoke.

"Wait a minute. Are you saying you think you heard the guy who called your cell phone? What was that about the governor?" Jason's voice was alert.

"The voice I heard sounds exactly the same as the governor's voice," Aubree repeated.

She heard papers rustling and Jason mumbling, and then he asked, "Where did you hear his voice?"

"It was on TV just now. He was giving a speech on some kind of farming legislation he's trying to pass." Aubree could hardly believe what she was saying. Jason would probably think she was delusional.

Jason hesitated. "The governor? I can look into this, but before I do, how sure are you about this?"

It was a question she had anticipated. Her palms were sweating, and her throat felt thick as she swallowed. "When I heard his voice, it was like—" She paused and took a breath. "It was like I was back in my car again, answering Devin's cell phone. His laugh even sounded the same."

Jason swore, and she heard him click his tongue. "I'm going to run some searches and get a recording of his voice. We'll do some checking and see if we can find anything linking him to the leads we've been investigating."

"What if you don't find anything?"

"If there's something to be found, we'll find it," Jason assured her. "I don't want you to worry. Just keep doing what you're doing and take care of yourself."

"Okay." Aubree tried to keep her voice from trembling.

"I'll contact you when I have more information," Jason said.

She closed her phone and slumped back against the couch. At best, her information would sound far-fetched, but at least Jason appeared to be taking her seriously—unless he was just trying to calm her down. She hoped for the best and wondered what the rest of the FBI would think when they were told to find dirt on Nebraska's governor.

Aubree knelt on the floor next to Scarlett, who gave her a toothless smile.

"Should we make some dinner?" Aubree asked and scooped up her chubby baby. At least she could pretend everything was normal, for now.

Fourteen

* * *

A WEEK HAD PASSED SINCE Aubree had contacted Jason, and she'd been jumpy ever since. She'd only left the house once and had watched every suspicious-looking vehicle closely in her rearview mirror. The past three nights, she'd reviewed all the training she'd received and reminded herself what to watch for. Even though she hadn't noticed anything different, she felt on edge.

Yesterday, she'd checked and rechecked the emergency bags she'd packed and stowed away in the SUV in case Jaybird ever told her to leave the nest. She smiled when she thought of the funny phrasing Jason would use if he ever felt her situation was too dangerous to stay in the house.

Adding a few more items to the emergency arsenal gave her something to do, but it didn't ease her mind. If the code was ever called, she would have to leave and head to a safe house where she would be re-routed again. She prayed the case would be solved before it ever came to that.

Aubree gave Scarlett one last bite of pureed squash, and the baby giggled and smeared the food across her face. Before Aubree could get her cleaned up, her cell phone rang. She jumped up and grabbed it. Her pulse raced when she read Jaybird on her caller ID. "Hello, this is Jolynn."

"Jaybird here with some information." Jason's voice was brisk, and Aubree sank back into her chair.

"Did you find anything?"

"Governor Ferrin is squeaky clean. I'm sorry, but we haven't found a trace of anything that would link him to this case. We're trying to tread carefully, though, and we're checking out all connections."

Aubree leaned her head into her hand and sighed. She watched Scarlett playing with the orange squash splatters on her tray. "So, I guess everything stays the same for now?"

"Yes," Jason said. "But we may come up with something yet."

"I guess that's why they call you guys the FBI," Aubree said.

"We'll keep trying to live up to our title," he said. "We're being very thorough. We'll be double-checking to see if there are any known criminals the governor has come in contact with. I'll call you next week and let you know what we find."

"Thanks," Aubree said and closed her cell phone. She felt restless as she digested the news Jason had given her. "Let's go to the store and get our groceries, Scarlett. I guess we're safe after all."

Scarlett smiled and waved her hands in the air. Aubree cleaned her up, grabbed the list off the fridge, and headed for the door. Maybe a quick shopping trip would relax her nerves.

As she pulled out of her driveway, Aubree noticed a pile of thorny sticks she had pruned from her rosebushes and frowned. She kept forgetting to get them disposed of even though they had sat there for over a month.

When the snow had finally retreated, and spring was near, she'd spent quite a bit of time working in the yard. The roses near the driveway were overgrown and hadn't been pruned for some time. It had taken a thick pair of leather gloves and a long-sleeved shirt to tackle the job. The thorns even made their way through her gloves at times. But with the help of the June sunshine, the roses had exploded into all kinds of beautiful blossoms. Now that it was almost July, Aubree made a mental note to get the pile of sticks by her front door taken care of today; the thorns could hurt someone if they tripped along her sidewalk.

"I'll have to cut some of those roses for our table," she said to Scarlett as they drove. Scarlett was happy to ride in the grocery cart, and the shopping trip was uneventful, but that's how Aubree preferred it. After checking off everything on her list, the back of the SUV was full of groceries and supplies she needed for the rest of the month. At least she didn't have to worry about money.

Jason had made it clear that all of her needs, within a reasonable amount, would be met by the program for the first year. Money was deposited into her account each month disguised as a paycheck. Her dear husband overseas took good care of them. At least that's what everyone in her neighborhood thought.

Glancing behind her, she noticed that Scarlett had fallen asleep. She pulled into the garage and waited for the noisy door to close before she got out of the car. She popped the hatch of the SUV; she could unload the car while Scarlett slept. She grabbed her purse and unlocked the door.

When she crossed the threshold, the hairs on the back of her neck stood up. She stepped softly into the kitchen and looked around. Something wasn't right, but what was it? She hurriedly punched in the code on her alarm, noting that it hadn't been disarmed.

Turning slowly, she listened for a sound that didn't belong. There was a slight rustle coming from the living room. Aubree's heart hammered in her chest as she walked around the corner. Part of her wanted to turn around and run, but then she remembered how jumpy she'd been the last week about every strange noise. She took another tentative step forward and peered into the living room. Nothing seemed out of place, but then her breath caught in her throat when a light breeze wafted through the open window.

Aubree whirled around and dug her hand into her purse, searching frantically for her cell phone. She pushed the speed dial and backed up slowly, straining her ears for any sound. There was nothing out of place in the kitchen or living room, and Aubree couldn't see any sign of movement down the hallway. Her heart was pounding, and she gasped when Jason answered.

"Jaybird, I just got home from the store, and there was a window open in my living room," she whispered.

"Has your alarm been deactivated?" Jason's voice rose slightly, and it made her all the more nervous.

She walked back through the kitchen toward the alarm panel. "I entered the code when I got home." She fished in her purse and pulled her pepper spray out, trying to ignore the blood beating in her ears.

"I can check from here to see when the code was entered last." Jason said. "It'll take a few minutes. Are you sure you didn't leave the window open?"

Aubree squeezed her eyes shut. "I don't remember opening it."

"Do you see any sign of an intruder?"

"No, but I'm scared."

"I'll send an officer over there for you. I want you to get back in your car and drive around the block."

"Scarlett's asleep in the car," Aubree said. "Maybe I'm just being paranoid. I think if someone were here they would've come out by now."

"I don't think you have anything to worry about, but I've got dispatch sending an officer over," Jason said. "Are you heading back to your car?"

Aubree glanced down the hallway and frowned. "Yes."

"I'm glad you called me. I'll have the alarm information for you soon to double check. We should be able to see when that window was opened."

"I don't remember opening it, and something didn't feel right when I came home," Aubree tried to explain. She took a few steps down the hall, noting that her bedroom door was closed as she had left it.

"I know it's hard not to worry, but you're hidden," Jason said. "No one even has a picture of what you look like right now. There's no record of the changes we made to your appearance."

"But what about the one in my file?"

"What? That doesn't look like you now. That's from when you were seven months pregnant with blonde hair," Jason said.

Aubree stopped near the front room, her breath catching in her throat at the memory of something that now exploded in her worried mind. "No, the one Miranda—Agent Olsen—took of me right after they dyed and cut my hair." Aubree heard a choking sound from the other end of the phone. "Jason?"

"Jaybird says leave the nest! Get out! Get out now!" Jason shouted.

The room seemed to tilt, and Aubree couldn't concentrate. Jason's voice was echoing in her ears as she tried to remember what she was supposed to do next. She stepped back and looked at the open window in the living room again. A thousand different thoughts buzzed through her mind. She looked at the pepper spray in her hand at the same instant the front door burst open.

Aubree screamed as a man barreled toward her. She raised the pepper spray and shot it directly at his face.

Her attacker hollered and stopped, but Aubree rapidly came alive. She ran at the man with all her might and pushed him. He was already backing away because of the pepper spray, and her momentum sent him flying. He tripped off the front steps and landed in the pile of rose clippings with jagged thorns, howling in agony.

Aubree didn't hesitate. She slammed the door and ran back through the house into the garage, coughing on the pepper spray that lingered in the air. She closed the hatch on the car and jumped inside, locking the doors. She put on her seat belt and opened the garage door. Behind her, Scarlett was still sleeping soundly. Aubree put the car into reverse and jammed her foot on the gas pedal.

She saw a flash of the dark jacket the man wore and heard a thump from the side of her vehicle. The tires screeched as she pulled onto the street and shifted the car into drive. The man lay unmoving on her driveway, and at first Aubree wondered if she'd run him over, but then she figured he'd run into the side of her car while trying to stop her. She sped down the street looking constantly in her rearview mirror.

During one glance, she noticed her own reflection. Mascara ran down her face, and she wiped at it, not even realizing she'd been crying. Her hands shook, and she gripped the steering wheel tighter. She willed herself to slow down as she headed for the nearest freeway entrance.

A buzzing sound from her purse made her heart jump. She fished out her cell phone and saw that Jason had just been trying to reach her. She glanced in her rearview mirror again as she pulled onto the freeway and dialed Jason's number.

"Aubree, are you okay?"

"I don't know. I think so," she stammered. "A man came through my front door. He was going to attack me—I used my pepper spray. I got away, and I'm driving on the freeway now," she said.

"The local police are on their way. I need a description to relay to them." Jason said.

"He was wearing a dark jacket. He was around six feet tall, maybe two hundred and twenty pounds," Aubree said. "I don't know. It happened so fast. I think he had dark hair and a mustache."

"That's good. Can you think of anything else that might make him stand out in a crowd?" Jason said.

"Not right now." Aubree tapped the steering wheel. "I'll keep thinking."

"Hold on a minute," he said. Aubree heard him give out the description and then he came back on the line. "Are you headed for the safe house?"

"Yes," she answered, but then hesitated. "How did they find me?"

"I'm trying to figure that out. It doesn't make sense. Something's wrong. They bypassed the security system."

She pursed her lips and then blew out her breath in a huff. "I don't think I'll go to the safe house after all."

"What? Aubree, you have to. It's the only way we can protect you."

"Maybe you'd better see who Agent Olsen shared her pictures with before I do that." Aubree felt her anger rise to the surface as she realized how close she'd come to losing her life.

"We've already got her in custody," Jason said. "We'll find out what she was up to. I'm sorry. I had no idea she'd taken your picture. Why didn't you say so before?"

"Because I trusted her. She had what seemed a legitimate reason to take my picture, and then I forgot about it."

"That was too close. You've got to come in, and we'll make sure you're safe," Jason said.

Aubree glanced at Scarlett in the back, still sleeping peacefully. She was headed to the safe house, but as the mile markers on the freeway whizzed past, she shook her head. "I'm not coming back in to be guarded day and night under house arrest, Jason."

She heard him swear in frustration. "It's the only way we can keep you alive."

"No!" Aubree slammed her hand against the steering wheel. "You can keep me alive by figuring out who is behind all this and putting them in prison. Until that happens, I'll never be safe. Your own agents have turned against you. Maybe you should look at what's happening right under your nose."

Jason swore again, but then he said, "Please. I've hardly slept since last week. I've been trying to find something on Governor Ferrin. I think we're closer than we know—we must be for them to come after you like this."

"I need time to think about what to do. I'll let you know."

"Please. Don't do something stupid."

"I won't," Aubree said, and she ended the call. Jason was sure the FBI could keep her safe, but she wasn't anymore. Whoever was behind this was too powerful. She approached the exit to the safe house. She glanced in her rearview mirror again and pressed on the gas pedal.

FIFTEEN

✳ ✳ ✳

A S SHE PASSED THE exit sign, Aubree's chest constricted, but she sucked in a breath of air and kept driving. Her attacker's face kept flashing before her eyes. She prayed silently as she drove and tried to think of a plan to stay alive. She had already lost Devin; she was determined to be there for Scarlett. The shock was wearing off, and her tremors subsided, but she kept the needle on the speedometer as high as she dared to get away from Omaha as fast as possible.

Aubree felt tired and hungry, but she kept driving for more than two hours as Scarlett slept. Around four in the afternoon, Scarlett woke up.

"I know you're hungry, sweetie. We'll stop soon, and I'll feed you." She tried to soothe Scarlett by singing softly. They had been heading south from Omaha, and the next city coming up was a small town called Aurora. The signs on the interstate indicated Aurora had hotels and restaurants, and yet she wondered if they should stop.

Scarlett wailed louder as Aubree slowed the car and exited the freeway. She pulled into the lot of the first grocery store she found and parked the car. Climbing into the backseat, she unbuckled Scarlett. Feeling grateful for tinted windows, she fed her baby and tried to think what to do next.

The air conditioner blew on her and rustled the grocery sacks in the back. Aubree said a quick prayer of thanks that she still had her groceries. She had just purchased new diapers, wipes, and baby food for Scarlett that afternoon. She had a good stock of food on hand. With a few other essentials, a cooler, and some ice, she could make it for several days on her own. Aubree's head snapped up as a thought came into her mind. She remembered all the fun experiences she'd had camping with her parents when she was young. She'd loved being outdoors where things were so secluded, away from anything and everyone.

By the time she finished feeding Scarlett, her mind was racing with the details of her new plan. If it worked, Aubree felt sure she could keep them safe until things settled down with the FBI. She reached over the backseat and pulled out a bag of bagels. Ripping pieces off a blueberry bagel, she chewed slowly while she thought of where to go next. Scarlett was content again for the time being, but she'd also need some solid baby food within an hour.

"I think we'll have to go shopping later for some more supplies," Aubree said to her baby. Scarlett just babbled in reply. Aubree drove slowly through the small town of Aurora until a sign caught her eye. She'd been looking for an outdoor supply store, but a small billboard announced, "Revolutionize your summer vacation! Buy your RV, trailer, SUV, in under an hour!"

She scanned the lot and then pulled into a parking space across the street. There were camping trailers, motor homes, pickups, and SUVs of all kinds for sale in a small lot. Aubree gazed out at the parking lot, her anxiety building as she considered how dangerous it might be to get out of the car.

After taking a few deep breaths, she climbed out of her car and retrieved her emergency bag from the back. She brought it around to the front seat and climbed back inside, locking the door. She looked around the parking lot again, but didn't notice anything suspicious.

She tugged on the zipper and pulled out a smaller bag. The bag contained several hundred-dollar bills, and Aubree flipped through them, checking the amount. It was more cash than she'd ever held in her life. Ten thousand dollars—the money came from Devin's life insurance policy. It wasn't a large policy, but it had covered burial expenses, and Aubree had put some in a special savings account under Scarlett's name. She had taken the rest with her.

Jason had given strict instructions on how she should pack her emergency bag, complete with a passport for Jolynn Dobson and money in case he decided she should leave the country. But she wasn't going to leave the country—that might be expected. Instead she was going somewhere no one would expect a city girl from San Diego to hide out. Aubree put the bag of money inside her purse's zipper compartment.

"You ready to go shopping?" She smiled at Scarlett and carefully draped a blanket over her head. Scarlett snuggled against her chest, and Aubree walked across the street to the RV lot. She stepped around several potholes in the cracked asphalt and eyed a dingy trailer positioned near the road.

This was a small town business, but if it could get her outfitted in an hour like the billboard said, it was worth a shot. Within a few seconds, a salesman with red hair and a gold hoop in one ear came out of the building.

"Are you looking for a vacation vehicle?" he asked and flashed a bleached smile.

"Yes," Aubree said. "I'm looking for a camping trailer and a pickup to pull it."

His eyes lit up, and he ran a hand through his curly hair. "Let me show you what we have." His cowboy boots crunched along the asphalt, and he pointed toward a group of used trailers.

She followed him around the lot as he showed her a few different models. She stopped in front of a fifteen-foot trailer and read the specs on a paper hanging from an inside window: Twelve years old and in good condition. "I'd like to look inside."

"Sure. This one's an older model, but it has all the amenities." He opened the door and motioned for her to step inside.

Scarlett cooed and reached out to grab the blue curtains hanging over the sink. Aubree shifted her to the other hip and opened a few of the cupboards. "There are dishes in here." She smiled in surprise.

"Yeah, we just acquired this, and it comes with pots and pans and the works." He opened another cupboard and pointed at a heap of old camping supplies. "The owners bought a brand new RV and said they were buying everything new to furnish it."

"Hmm, that's perfect for me," Aubree said. She walked to the front of the trailer and examined the couch.

"That doubles as a bed when folded out," the salesman said. "The dining table also converts to a bed for two,"

Aubree peeked inside the tiny bathroom. It had a small bathtub with a showerhead in the corner. "Is it hard to empty the waste water?"

"Come outside, and I'll show you. This one's been fitted with some new hoses to make it easier." He stepped down from the trailer. "We also have a copy of the owner's manual, which comes in handy."

Aubree listened while he told her how to put clean water in the tank and empty the waste. She asked several questions and tried to memorize all of his answers.

The price on the trailer was marked at $4,800. Looking around the lot, she noticed a blue Ford pickup. "How old is that truck? It looks kind of beat up." She saw a dent in the driver's side door and one on top of the hood.

"That one comes with its own memories. It's fourteen years old but only has 125,000 miles." They walked to the pickup as he told her about some of the damage to the body. "It runs great, but since its appearance hasn't been kept up, we're only asking $2,500 for it."

Aubree looked the pickup over and climbed inside to start it up. The salesman showed her some things to look for under the hood. Even with his salesman smile, he was proving to be more helpful than she'd hoped. She didn't know much about pickups; she just needed something reliable. This pickup was old enough that she wouldn't have to worry about air bags in the front seat, as Scarlett would have to ride beside her. After looking at a few other pickups and trailers, Aubree made the salesman an offer. "I'd like to take the camp trailer and this pickup now for $6,000."

"I'm glad you like them, but that's a pretty low offer. Together they're $7,300, but I could knock off $500 for you." He smiled his white-toothed grin as Aubree did some calculating.

"I'll pay you $6,500 cash right now if you'll help me get hooked up and out of here." Aubree smiled as his eyes widened, but he kept his composure. She held out her hand.

He shook it. "Sounds like you're anxious to get some camping done before the summer's out."

"I want to be on my way this weekend." Aubree winked and then smiled at Scarlett. "It'll be her first camping trip."

Forty-five minutes later, she pulled her new camp trailer and pickup across the street into the parking lot of a grocery store. A kind of frenzied excitement gave her a buzz of energy, and she jotted down a list of things they might need. Then she put Scarlett in a grocery cart and pushed her into the store. One hour and a full grocery cart later, she pushed a grumpy Scarlett out to the trailer. She opened a bottle of baby peaches and fed her hungry baby.

"I'm sorry I made you wait so long," she told Scarlett. She noted that more time had passed than she'd realized. The hands on her watch reached closer to seven o'clock. She set Scarlett on the floor with a few toys and blankets and worked steadily to stock up her new trailer.

Aubree cleaned out her SUV of every scrap of paper and every detail that she had ever been inside. They would still find it, but she was determined that they wouldn't find her. She shook her head wondering who "they" really were. Who was she even running from? She took her cell phone out of her purse and made the call she'd been dreading all day. Jason picked up after the first ring.

"Aubree, where are you? I'm going out of my mind here!"

"Jason, listen to me. I trust you, but I don't trust the FBI right now."

"But—"

"No, I'm doing this my way," Aubree interrupted his protests. "I'll contact you again when I can."

"Please don't throw your life away like this," Jason pleaded.

"Do you have any new information on my case?" Aubree demanded. "Did they find the guy who attacked me?"

Jason hesitated. "Not that I can share over the phone. And no, we're still looking for the suspect."

"Then I'm not throwing my life away. I'm taking control of it." She ran her fingers through her short dark hair. "Thank you for all you've done. I'm sorry to do this, but I have to think of Scarlett." She hung up before he could say any more, then tossed the phone onto the floor of her SUV and locked the doors. She felt a new surge of apprehension wash over her, but she forced herself to shrug it off.

Aubree marveled again at the good fortune of having all the groceries from her shopping trip earlier that day. It seemed like all of that had happened weeks ago, not hours. When she had put away as much as she could, she stopped to settle Scarlett in for the night. By eight o'clock, the baby was sleeping in her car seat in the old pickup, and Aubree was studying a map she had picked up at the grocery store.

She pulled out of the parking lot slowly, getting the feel of her new trailer as she drove. Her Realtor's office in San Diego had owned several nice trailers they used to help their clients move. Aubree had learned how to maneuver a trailer quite skillfully over the past few years. She was glad that she had gained such experience, or she would have never dreamed up what she was about to do. The entrance to Interstate 80 loomed before her, and she drove carefully, listening to the radio and running the details of her plan through her mind.

Two-hundred and thirty miles later, at fourteen minutes past midnight, the old blue pickup pulled into Sterling, Colorado. Aubree felt exhausted but happy to put so much distance between herself and Omaha. She found the North Sterling State Park, paid the camping fee, and pulled the trailer into an empty site. She fixed up the convertible couch in the trailer, and then moved Scarlett into the bed with her. With eyes squeezed shut, she concentrated on falling asleep before her mind began racing with worry.

✳ ✳ ✳

"Ma, ma, ma, ma, ma," Scarlett babbled happily and pulled Aubree's hair.

"Well, good morning to you too." Aubree giggled and kissed Scarlett's chubby cheeks. It was hard to believe her baby was just shy of nine months old. Aubree ruffled Scarlett's silky curls and glanced at her watch—six forty-five. It was pretty early, and she could've slept much longer, but they had a lot of miles to cover today.

Over breakfast, she studied the atlas and figured that with a stop somewhere for Scarlett's mid-morning snack, they should reach Steamboat Springs, Colorado, by about one o'clock. Before they left, she carried the box of hair dye she'd purchased the previous night into the restroom at the park.

It wasn't easy to dye her hair over a sink and keep Scarlett entertained in her car seat, but forty minutes later, Aubree emerged as a redhead. In the trailer, she brushed her "autumn leaf" hair away from her face. In a few months, it would be long enough to put in a ponytail. She had been due for a haircut but hadn't scheduled it yet. The hair was a few inches past her ears and barely approached the nape of her neck. She ran her fingers through Scarlett's dark curls and then cleaned up their breakfast mess.

After a few hours of driving, Aubree kept yawning and was glad that feeding Scarlett gave her a reason to stop. She dozed off while she nursed her baby in the trailer and awoke startled and disoriented a half hour later. She'd been dreaming. Or had it just been her mind racing? The dream had something to do with her mother, and Aubree longed to talk to her, but she knew she couldn't.

It wasn't difficult to think who Jason would've contacted right after she hung up on him yesterday. Her mom was probably sick with worry, but Aubree couldn't call and risk giving away her location. It was the only way she could be safe for now.

When the pickup was back on Highway 40, Aubree's mind returned to a thought she couldn't shake. It was really an idea, but if her idea proved correct, it might mean the end of all this running. After all, how long did she expect to live on the run? Aubree narrowed her eyes and pursed her lips, remembering what she'd told Jason—that she was taking control of her life. She glanced at Scarlett sleeping peacefully in her car seat. What other choice did she have?

SIXTEEN

✳   ✳   ✳

I'LL FIND HER." JASON slammed the phone down and looked at the files scattered across his desk. His director wanted to see results, not the lead witness in the Robert Walden assassination gone missing. He had to find Aubree—not just because his director wanted him to but because he was afraid if he didn't someone else would.

He flipped open a red file folder—his signature color for prime suspects—and looked at the contents he'd put together only hours earlier. Information was pointing in all directions, and he wasn't sure how many leaks he had to fill before Aubree would be safe. Rolling up his sleeves, he clenched his jaw and picked up the phone. "I need to be involved in the Miranda Olsen interrogation." He paused, "Yes, it's regarding the Aubree Stewart case—she's missing."

✳   ✳   ✳

After a short rest and a delicious Caesar salad in Steamboat Springs, Aubree and Scarlett resumed their travel and soon crossed over the Utah border. Opting to take the least traveled route possible, they steered clear of the interstates and sailed along Highway 40.

Scarlett babbled and played with the colorful rings hanging from her car seat. When she tired of that, she gave Aubree an earful of crying and then slept for long stretches. They passed through Vernal, Utah, and Aubree only had to stop a couple times among the desert and dinosaur monuments to change Scarlett's diaper and feed her.

At about six in the evening, Aubree reached Heber City and breathed a sigh of relief.

"We're almost there, baby," Aubree said. "Tomorrow, we'll do some real camping." They ate at a quiet restaurant, and Aubree watched people coming and going, listening to bits of their conversations.

"You going camping in the Uintas?" one man asked a guy decked out in hiking attire.

"Yeah. The trails should be good this time of year."

"Well, don't forget your slicker. It rains somewhere in those mountains every day of the year."

Aubree took note and later stopped at a general store to pick up a few more supplies, including a warm sleeping bag. She checked the tires of her pickup and trailer and found a small RV site not far from the restaurant. She hooked up to the water and decided to try out her new shower. It was a bit cramped, but at least she was clean. She even gave Scarlett a bath in the half size tub and laughed as Scarlett continually splashed the water and giggled.

"I think we're going to be okay, darlin'," Aubree said. She had hardly spoken to anyone all day and felt sure no one would be looking for her in a tiny Utah town called Heber City. She probably could've driven further that night, but the anxiety and worry from the day before and the strain from driving all day had completely exhausted her. She cuddled up next to Scarlett just after eight o'clock, and they both slept until the sun rose over the mountains.

Shaking off her nightmares, Aubree breathed in the cool mountain air filtering in through her trailer windows. Now that it was July, it would be plenty hot during the day, but the nights in the mountains would still be chilly. By seven-thirty in the morning, they were driving past beautiful three-story houses in Heber.

Thirty minutes later, she passed through the small town of Kamas. The old pick-up held its own on the steep ascents. She felt her ears pop and noticed the tops of mountain peaks getting closer. A simple one-lane road would be her path through the high Uinta Mountains. It was such a feeling of freedom to look out over pine trees and the shimmering quaking aspens and know that, right now, no one knew where she was.

The sun beamed down with only a few puffy white clouds, yet as she continued driving, the sunlight dipped behind gathering gray clouds, and the deserted highway suddenly glistened black with rain. The wipers on the truck struggled to keep up, and they screeched across the windshield as the droplets of rain continued to splat with a million different beats. Then—as abruptly as it had started—the rain stopped.

There was a remarkable difference from the extreme flatlands of Nebraska to the high summit called Bald Mountain she was driving by now. A huge skyline of jagged black peaks took her breath away. The pine trees bordered the road at eye level and were green enough that Aubree could almost forget she was in Utah.

The signs for several overlooks and small fishing lakes kept her attention. She passed Mirror Lake, Butterfly Lake, Pass Lake, and drove over the Bald Mountain pass. She was thrilled at the sight of a sign proclaiming Christmas Meadows and could hardly believe her eyes as she noted that the white patches along the road were actually snow—in July! Bits of mist hung in the air like lonesome clouds, and Aubree reveled in the solitude of the mountains.

A tingling sensation in her chest brought her back to the present, and she knew Scarlett would soon be waking to eat. She thought about the times so long ago that she and her parents had traveled through mountains to go camping, she was certainly more carefree then than she was now. If only the FBI could find the enemy stalking her, she thought. She rubbed her tongue over her teeth, considering what Jason had said a week ago. He was convinced she knew something important about the crime. And maybe he was right. Maybe, hidden under nightmarish voices and restless nights, Aubree's mind held the key to solving her own case.

Swallowing the idea, hoping to digest it later, she looked for the next area where she could safely pull off the road. A sign indicating a hiking trail and lake showed there was access for a trailer, and she pulled onto the dirt path carefully. There was only one other car in the area, and the morning dew still clung to the grasses growing haphazardly around the trailhead.

Aubree thanked heaven again that she was able to acquire her trailer as she relaxed into the cushions of the couch to feed Scarlett. She concentrated on pleasant thoughts of the road ahead and hoped she could find just the right campground to stay for a time and feel safe. Her final destination would be close to the source of those good memories she recalled of camping with her family.

She awoke forty-five minutes later feeling a bit of chagrin but shrugged it off.

"We're making good time, and I'd much rather fall asleep with you than on the road," she whispered to Scarlett. Aubree grabbed a few snacks for her and the baby, and after a quick look at the pristine lake, they were on their way again.

Once they left the rich forests of the Uintas, the drive became considerably less intriguing. The mountains opened up to flat, treeless plains, and there would not be another city to see until they reached Evanston, Wyoming, around lunchtime. They'd be there in less than an hour, but Aubree already felt eager to get back to more interesting scenery.

Her thoughts were on what to order for lunch when she glanced in the rearview mirror. A car was approaching rapidly. Aubree checked her speed to make sure she wasn't impeding traffic. Her pickup held steady at sixty miles per hour, and she figured the other driver must be in a hurry. Luckily, the road wasn't busy, and the car could pass her easily. Only it didn't.

The maroon car edged closer until it was tailgating her trailer. It looked like there were two people in the car, and as they continued to cling to her bumper, Aubree panicked. Had they found her already? She hated that she didn't even know what her enemy looked like. She wondered if she should tap on her brakes or just pull over—but then what if that was what they wanted her to do?

"Maybe coming through these back roads wasn't such a bright idea," she mumbled to herself. She glanced over at Scarlett, who was happily sucking on a teething ring, and knew she would do anything to keep her safe.

Another look in the rearview mirror showed that the car was still uncomfortably close. She could see there were definitely two men inside, but they looked older from a distance. Perhaps they were just some fishermen too caught up in a big fish story to pay attention to their bad driving.

After five miles, they were still tailgating her. Aubree slowed down to ten miles under the speed limit. Her hands shook, and she kept wondering if she should pull over or speed up. Then the car suddenly zoomed past her. The men didn't even look her way.

Aubree almost cried in relief as she watched the car speed further ahead. She was angry at herself for getting scared. The faceless enemy was her worst nightmare. That cackling voice from her dreams lurked behind every unfriendly male she came in contact with.

She felt unsettled again when she approached some construction just before Evanston. She imagined someone hijacking her pickup while she waited for the man wearing the dirty orange vest to twirl his stop sign back around like some kind of crazy dance prop. She willed herself to stay calm and mentally begged the sign to turn. Every large group of rocks was another hiding place for an enemy to hide. By the time she pulled into a gas station in Evanston, her nerves were taut, and her emotions were swirling out of control.

She fueled her pickup, paid cash for her gas, bought some lunch, and then pulled into a larger parking lot and retreated to her trailer. Aubree focused her attention on feeding Scarlett and took several deep cleansing breaths to relax her strained mental state. *No one knows where I am, not even Jason*, she thought, and she repeated it several times over. She picked up her atlas and consulted the map of Idaho again. She also looked at a smaller booklet with lists of campsites around the Bear Lake area. It was the same location she and her family had camped in, and the feelings of security and good memories had led her back. She only hoped it was the right choice.

An hour later, the old pick-up rounded a bend, and Bear Lake came into view. It spread out before her, a mass of cool blue reflecting the sky above it. As she drove down into the valley, Aubree noticed the large number of RVs, tents, boats, jet skis, and all kinds of recreational vehicles.

She drove past the south beach and continued to journey northward. The color of the lake was like a chameleon—changing shades of blue from deep azure in the middle to an almost turquoise hue near the beach. Seagulls dotted the shoreline, and the beach sand, rocks, and grasses mingled along the water's edge. Bear Lake was so large it crossed into Idaho from Utah, and Aubree's plan was to head to the Idaho border.

Driving past rows and rows of condominiums, an entire marina of sailboats, and more camping areas, Aubree smiled to herself. A person could get lost among all the campers, tents, and trailers, and that was exactly what she intended to do. Twenty miles later, she had still not reached the northern side of Bear Lake. She continued driving and saw signs indicating the small towns surrounding the area. Paris, Idaho, was only fifteen miles away. Few cars traveled the road as she left the lake behind her and headed toward the tiny town.

"Here we go, Scarlett, only a few more miles now," Aubree said cheerfully. She had selected a small, out-of-the-way camping area and hoped it would prove to be a good one. She turned left off the highway in Paris and navigated a dusty, washboard road. The five miles to the campground seemed more like twenty as she traveled the winding road at fifteen miles per hour.

Just when she questioned if she had made a wrong turn, she came upon the campground of Paris Springs. Tucked back into a remote area surrounded by a creek and river willows, the campground exuded peacefulness. She stopped at the self-serve reservation area and paid cash for three nights. Tucking the slip into her dashboard, Aubree hoped the camp host wouldn't wonder too much when she asked to reserve a spot for the next few weeks.

The campsites formed a large circle, and Aubree drove about halfway around it before she reached site fourteen. She jumped out of the truck and looked for the best place to park so that her trailer would be level. The road had been graded and looked pretty smooth, so she pulled the trailer in and parked her truck.

The salesman had given her a tip sheet on how to park a trailer. She looked it over and then selected a few large rocks to put around the wheels. Following his other instructions, she set up her trailer for a "safe and enjoyable camping experience." Then she took Scarlett inside and prepared their first meal in the Paris Springs Campground.

Rubbing the fatigue and worry from his eyes, Jason pulled up beside the green SUV in the grocery store parking lot. He felt exhausted after jetting to Omaha and speeding to Aurora—the last place he knew of Aubree's whereabouts.

He climbed out of his vehicle and used a Slim Jim to break into Aubree's car. He cursed when he saw the light reflecting off the silver phone on the floor. Slumping into the driver's seat, he popped the cover off the phone and carefully removed the battery and transmitter. It had been nearly twenty-four hours since he'd begged Aubree to come to the safe house.

When the transmitting signal stayed in the same area overnight, he figured she had checked into a motel. He let the transmitter fall to the asphalt outside the door and then ground it to tiny shards with his heel. He'd underestimated Aubree Stewart. She'd abandoned this cell phone and broken all ties with him. She was on her own now. He stood and glanced around the parking lot, noting the small stores surrounding the perimeter. His eyes narrowed when he saw a bright billboard in front of a used car lot—"Revolutionize your summer vacation! Buy your RV, trailer, SUV, in under an hour!"

✳ ✳ ✳

After a simple dinner of a sandwich Aubree had purchased at the grocery store, she tidied up the trailer and examined the contents of the cupboards. She had everything needed to cook several meals. Aubree felt apprehensive about using the little stove but figured she didn't have many other options besides cooking over a fire. *Too bad I'm not a Dutch oven expert like Uncle Keith*, she thought as she rummaged around the miscellaneous pots and pans.

"I guess I'll try something simple first, like eggs." She tickled Scarlett. "How would you like eggs for breakfast tomorrow?"

Scarlett giggled and then babbled, "Ma, ma, ma, ma."

Aubree changed Scarlett's clothes and decided it might be a good idea to check out the campground. Trading her sandals for a pair of tennis shoes from her emergency bag, she scanned the area and then carefully locked the trailer door. The campground had a dirt road circling the area. She pushed Scarlett in a pink and blue umbrella stroller and smiled as her baby jabbered nonsense about the new scenery.

They walked around the big loop of the campground. There were several smaller campsites like hers and two that were much larger, with space for up to twenty campers. She suspected that the weekends would probably be busy. The campground was only about half-full, and she didn't notice a camp host anywhere.

As they rounded the bend to return to their campsite, Aubree saw a sign marking a trailhead for Paris Springs. The path looked quiet and beautiful with the sun slanting through the quaking aspens that lined the grassy trail. She made a mental note to find out where the trail led and whether or not it would be possible to carry Scarlett. Her chunky daughter was thriving, and Aubree knew she couldn't hike for long with a twenty-pound baby on her hip.

Aubree's thoughts returned to her current situation. During her drive from Nebraska, Aubree had gone over every detail she knew about the case in her head. Everything Jason had told her pointed to a chink in the FBI's impenetrable armor. Someone from the inside knew a lot about her, and Aubree didn't think that person was Miranda Olsen. It would've been too easy for Miranda to harm her while she was staying at the safe house in Los Angeles.

Aubree shook her head as she thought about the facts. Miranda was a pawn in somebody's game, and the real players remained hidden with someone's help on the inside. Aubree still felt that the voice of the governor of Nebraska was the same as the one she'd heard nearly a year ago, but she'd have to find a way to prove it before she and Scarlett could ever feel safe.

Later that night, Aubree snuggled with Scarlett in the old trailer. She held her baby under the safe canopy of forest pine trees where there was no cell phone service and where there was no chance of getting a wrong number.

SEVENTEEN

* * *

"WE NEED TO FIND her undercover and watch her undercover," Jason said. "Find someone who can go on a road trip." He gripped his cell phone, and his fingers strayed to the gun in his holster. "Keep her mom on the radar. I think Aubree's too smart to go there, but we can't be sure." He pushed the end key on the call and blew out a breath of frustration. The FBI couldn't employ its usual tactics to find a missing person in the hunt for Aubree. If they put her picture on the news, then the assassins would know what she looked like now and that she wasn't in hiding.

As if the search wasn't complicated enough, only a select team of agents was able to take part in the hunt for Aubree because of the compromised security at the FBI. Until the Bureau could find the source of the leak, Jason's team was communicating on a need-to-know basis.

His supervisor, Agent Napierski, had reassured him that they'd find her. "A fifteen-foot trailer can't travel incognito," he'd said, and Jason agreed, but Aubree had the advantage of a great head start, and there were thousands of campgrounds between Colorado and Idaho—if that was even where she was headed. He slammed his hand on the bedside table of the hotel. What if she'd headed east instead of west? He had to find her before it was too late.

* * *

The next few days were uneventful, yet peaceful, as Aubree and Scarlett roamed the campground. She finally found a camp chief who did the scheduling for several campgrounds and reserved her spot for the next sixteen days, which was the limit. Then, just to be on the safe side, she reserved another spot for a full sixteen days more.

He filled out her reservation slips and handed them to her. "Quite the camper, eh?"

"Just making up for lost time. I've been working too hard," Aubree said.

"Well, you'll have a good stretch here." He spat on the ground. "There's a park ranger that comes through about once a day. He can show you what wood you can use for fires. Sometimes he collects the deadfall and distributes it."

"That'd be great. Can you tell me about the trailhead I saw?"

"Paris Springs? It's our namesake here, and it's a beauty." He pointed to the far end of the campground. "It's about a half-mile walk to see the natural spring coming out of the mountains."

"Is it very steep?" Aubree glanced at Scarlett and smiled.

"Nah, you should be able to tote her along. You should give it a try."

"I think I will. Thanks for your help." Aubree held onto the slips of paper and shifted Scarlett to her hip.

"Enjoy your stay." The camp chief waved, and Aubree watched him amble down the road.

The Paris Springs Campground was quiet, and even though it was mid-July, temperatures dropped at night. There wasn't much for Aubree to do besides keep the trailer tidy and care for Scarlett. At first, she tried to forget about the wrong number and the murders connected to it, but Jason's insistence that she must know more than she realized kept tugging at the strings of her memory. She began jotting down notes about all the people she had worked with during the investigation, and she wondered who she could trust. Was Jason leak proof?

And then she thought about Devin. Aubree had been angry with Devin for a long time after she moved to Nebraska. It was still hard to think about her misplaced trust in him and the problems he had with Internet gambling. Sometimes she questioned how much he had really loved her. Gradually, her feelings of anger had dissipated, and Scarlett had become a concrete reminder of the good things she'd shared with Devin. Aubree often felt alone and scared, but she wouldn't allow herself to wallow in regret.

When she'd unpacked her emergency bag, she'd found the notebook from her mother sealed in a manila envelope to hide her identity. Aubree was grateful she had kept the notebook in a safe spot.

Now, as she read from the pages, a soothing feeling warmed her heart, and she knew it was time to forgive Devin and let him go. Madeline had encouraged her to cherish her memories of her husband. Aubree's heart had been through more emotional trauma in the last year than in the whole rest of her life. Aubree felt determined that she wouldn't let her circumstances affect Scarlett. It would be up to her to give her baby a good life—one that was happy and, hopefully, safe.

After spending just over a week in the campground, Aubree began to feel the tightness and tension around her heart dissolve. She still didn't let her guard down—she checked each new arrival at the campground for signs of suspicious behavior—but she couldn't help enjoying the knowledge that no one knew where she was.

Darkness fell around the campsite, and Scarlett slept peacefully on the sofa bed as Aubree consulted her notebook of case details. The crickets chirped in rhythm, and she listened to the beat, letting it permeate the fog of information running through her mind. Aubree rested her face in her hands but tensed when she heard a strange noise. A scratching sound just outside her trailer sent her pulse into a staccato dance.

Holding her breath, she glanced out the tiny windows into the darkness. She heard a slight rustle and another scratching noise. Aubree felt like a cornered rabbit inside the dimly lit trailer surrounded by the dark forest. Scrambling for a flashlight, she moved closer to the door and listened. The movement outside and the strange scratching sounds continued. Aubree gripped the flashlight so tightly her fingers hurt.

Someone was out there in the dark wandering around her campsite. She didn't know if she should scream for help, but surely whoever it was had already seen her sitting at the table under the dim trailer light. Glancing at the sleeping form of her baby, she clicked on the flashlight and pointed it toward the screen door.

A chattering erupted, and eyes glowed white in the darkness. Aubree lunged forward and opened the door as recognition flashed through her brain. She pointed the flashlight at the source of the noise—a striped tail swished in and out of the beam of light. The raccoon chattered again, and he and his comrades scampered away into the darkness.

Aubree sank onto the threshold of the trailer and laughed. Her body trembled with the adrenaline that had rushed through her and now dissipated. She rubbed her hands on her arms. A few twinkling stars blinked through the canopy of trees overhead, and the moon illuminated bits of scattered trash from the raccoons in her campsite. She climbed back into the trailer and shoved her notebook in a corner before preparing for bed. If her only fear were raccoons in the night, she might be able to sleep soundly for once.

"I think it's time for us to check out that trail," Aubree said to Scarlett the next day after the baby had eaten her mid-morning snack. Scarlett waved her arms and smiled. They had been cooped up in her trailer hiding from unknown enemies for long enough. Aubree hoped that enough time had passed that she could venture farther from her trailer and still be safe.

Aubree rubbed bug spray and sunscreen on herself and Scarlett and slung the diaper bag over her shoulder. She wondered if the umbrella stroller could make the trail but decided she would just have to carry her plump baby. Now nearly nine months old, Scarlett was already starting to pull herself up to things, and Aubree guessed it wouldn't be much longer before she attempted to walk.

"Pretty soon you'll weigh as much as a bag of sugar." Aubree kissed Scarlett's cheek. "Good thing you're just as sweet." She ran her fingers through the dark curls and smiled into Scarlett's blue eyes. "Your hair is perfect. Let's fix mine." Aubree pinned the hair back away from her face. The dark auburn waves still surprised her, but the short style was growing out a little, and maybe eventually she could go back to her natural color. She checked that everything was secure in the trailer and locked the door. Then, with baby in tow, she headed for the Paris Springs Trailhead.

The summer sun was warm upon Aubree's back, and Scarlett tried to grab onto the leaves of overhanging branches as they started up the trail. The path sloped gently through the trees, barely clear of the encroaching bushes and wildflowers. The trail rose higher at one point, and when Aubree reached the peak of the hill, she found a rock to sit on to rest for a minute.

Her arms tingled from the pressure of holding Scarlett, and she rolled her shoulders back and glanced at the downhill slope ahead.

She heard a friendly whistle coming along the trail and looked up just as a park ranger crested the hill. He didn't see her until he was almost passing her, and he choked on the tune coming from his throat.

"Oh, hello there," he said. His cheeks were pink, either from hiking or being surprised.

"Good morning," Aubree said.

"You must be headed up to the springs." He pointed his thumb behind him and leaned his arm against a tree. He was quite tall, and because she was sitting, he seemed even taller.

"Yes, is it much further?"

"Nope, and it's pretty much downhill from here. You're over halfway there." He smiled, and Aubree noticed how his hazel eyes twinkled. "There's not as much water coming down this time of year, but it's still quite a sight."

Aubree stood and hefted Scarlett onto her hip. "Thanks. I've been wanting to check it out."

"Enjoy yourself." He reached out and patted Scarlett's cheek. "She sure is a cutie. I guess your arms will be tired, but there are plenty of places to sit up there and not too many people right now either."

Aubree gave him a stiff smile. It was difficult for her to act normal around people, and she'd had to concentrate to keep from flinching when he'd reached for Scarlett. It would take some time to undo the programmed anxiety she'd developed toward every person she'd met over the last year.

"That's good to know," Aubree responded. She stepped forward on the trail and clutched her baby closer. "See ya."

"Yep, have a good one," he said and continued down the trail.

Aubree walked a few more paces and then heard the cheerful whistle start up again. She turned and watched the retreating figure of the park ranger with the wavy brown hair.

The rushing sounds of water grew louder with every step she took along the trail. She was closer to the small creek now, and up ahead, large boulders surrounded the water. Soon she heard the cascading gurgles of the spring rise up to meet them as they reached the end of the dirt path.

"Scarlett, it's beautiful. Look at the water." Aubree pointed to a series of small waterfalls gushing over the rocks. Her voice was swallowed up in the roar of the spring, and her skin tingled as the air dropped in temperature near the icy water.

She picked her way carefully through the rocky path and found a large boulder to sit on. Then she pulled Scarlett's silky blanket out of the diaper bag and tucked it around her. Leaning back on the rock, she inhaled the crisp, clean air deeply. Scarlett was fascinated by the noisy water, and she squealed.

There wasn't another person in sight, and as Aubree glanced up the trailhead, she noted that she probably wouldn't hear anyone this close to the spring anyway. The water cascading down the mountain was almost musical, and she closed her eyes for a few moments, basking in the peacefulness of the area. When Scarlett started to fidget, Aubree slid off the rock and helped her wiggle her fingers in the icy cold water.

As she stepped back from the spring, she noticed a black camera bag sitting between two rocks. She picked it up, wondering if she should open the bag to try to discover who the owner was. Scarlett reached for the bag and cooed.

"Oh, you found it!" a voice behind her called.

Aubree jumped and spun around. "Oh!" The park ranger from earlier stood a few feet from her. "Is this yours?" She held out the camera bag, her heart racing.

"Yes. I didn't realize I'd left it here until I was nearly back to camp." He swung the camera over his shoulder. "Thanks. I didn't mean to scare you. The springs are pretty loud, huh?"

"They're beautiful," Aubree said. She licked her lips and tried to ignore the hammering heartbeat accompanying her startled nerves. She was aware that if this man wasn't really a park ranger, there would be no way to escape. Her apprehension must have been apparent on her face, because he cocked an eyebrow and smiled.

"I'm really sorry I startled you." He held out a rough, calloused hand. "I'm Wyatt Erickson. What's your name?"

Without thinking, she shook his hand and answered, "Aubree—" and then choked on her words.

Wyatt didn't seem to notice. "And is your husband back at camp?"

"My husband passed away about a year ago," Aubree stammered.

"I'm sorry. I shouldn't have—" Wyatt blushed and shook his head.

"Don't worry, it's—it's okay," Aubree said.

"Hey, could I walk with you back to camp?"

Aubree's throat constricted, but she found herself nodding. He hadn't reacted strangely when he heard her name, and although her training with the FBI screamed caution, her senses were at ease.

They began walking up the path, but Aubree's heart caught in her throat, and she stopped when she noticed a holster attached to his belt. "You have a gun?" She eyed the weapon hanging from his waist.

"I only carry it when I have to," Wyatt answered. He reached out and touched her arm. "Take it easy. There are a few campgrounds that get a little wild sometimes when people start drinking, and I'm the closest law enforcement. I just did the rounds at one of those and forgot to put away my firearm."

"But I didn't know—" Aubree was still staring at the gun. "I thought . . ."

"That I was just a park ranger?" Wyatt gave her a relaxed smile. "Park rangers do a whole heck of a lot more than people think. I went through the criminal justice program at Northwestern University in Colorado."

"Criminal justice?" Aubree raised her eyebrows. "I thought you guys just gave people tickets and cut firewood."

Wyatt laughed so hard he actually bent over and slapped his knee. "We do a lot more than most people would expect." He straightened up, and they resumed the hike back to the campground.

"Well, that's good, but criminal justice? I had no idea." Aubree shifted Scarlett onto her other hip.

"Can I carry her for you?" He extended his arms.

Aubree hesitated and looked at Scarlett. Could she trust this man? What if this was some kind of trap?

"Don't worry. All rangers are trained in first aid, and I'm actually an EMT."

"Really? I guess you can then." Aubree held her daughter toward him, and Scarlett surprised her by reaching for Wyatt. "So you're an EMT, too?" For some reason, Aubree believed him, and she didn't feel like she was in danger.

"Yeah, I help with search and rescue in the area, and I help with forest fires—if anyone gets hurt."

"How long did it take you to learn everything?"

Wyatt chuckled. "My mom tells me I could've been a doctor by now with all my schooling and training. It's taken me quite a while. I started going to school eight years ago, but I took a year off to build houses in Mexico." He shuffled one foot in the dirt. "I have a master's degree from Utah State. Then I did my EMT certification, law enforcement training, and a minor in photography." He grinned at her sheepishly.

Aubree gulped. She wondered if she should reveal more about herself or not. Wyatt had just told her all about himself and seemed expectant.

"I love photography. That was my major when I started college. I didn't finish though . . ." She trailed off.

"Photography is almost like an inborn talent. I bet you're still great. What's your favorite subject?"

"Well, I used to say landscapes, but ever since Scarlett was born I think it's been her."

Wyatt laughed. "I can see why. She's as pretty as her mother."

Aubree felt her cheeks burning, and her mind reeled as she tried to think of what to say. "I've been to Mexico. I helped on one of those humanitarian housing projects right after my freshman year of college." She didn't think it was possible for his smile to get any wider, but he proved her wrong.

"Awesome! We have something in common already."

Aubree couldn't help smiling back because even Wyatt's eyes seemed to be smiling now. "Guess so, but I didn't finish college." She looked down and kicked at a rock lodged in the dirt.

"Well, sometimes life throws us more curve balls than we expect."

She looked at him and bit her lip. She didn't know why her heart was hammering. She tried to think of what to say next, but she couldn't concentrate on anything but his hazel eyes.

"Ahh, Mexico." He said it with a strong accent. "Lots of sun and wonderful people there."

"I've only been the one time. But it was fun, I mean, *que divertido.*" Aubree turned toward the cool breeze blowing off the mountain, hoping it would hide the redness of her cheeks.

"Oh, *hables Español?*"

"No, no. *Un poquito.*"

Wyatt rattled off something in Spanish so fast that Aubree held up her hand. "No. I only know a little."

Wyatt shrugged. "Maybe I'll have to teach you some more."

"Well, here we are." She pointed at her campsite and reached for Scarlett. "I'd better go in and get her fed."

"Thanks for finding my camera bag and letting me carry this cute little lug," Wyatt said.

"My pleasure. Thanks for giving my arms a break." She stepped closer to her trailer.

"I'll be around if you need anything," Wyatt said.

"Um, thanks." Aubree walked back into her trailer and scolded herself for feeling so giddy. She looked in the mirror on the closet and saw that her face was flushed. She smiled in spite of herself. She couldn't help but notice the way Wyatt's eyes had fallen when she said they had to go. But she knew he was just overeager for conversation. It was his job to be friendly and help campers feel like coming again, right?

Leaning over the bed, she watched Scarlett play. She was so beautiful and healthy. The fat rolls extended all the way to her wrists, which were nonexistent, and her tiny hands were always reaching for something.

Aubree slumped down into the cushions surrounding the table. Maybe Wyatt wasn't just a park ranger. Her throat suddenly felt dry. What if they had found her? But Wyatt was too friendly—or was he trying to find out what she knew?

She had to keep Scarlett safe, no matter what. She couldn't let anything or anyone distract her. Leaning her head down to rest in her arms, she took a deep breath. This wasn't how she'd imagined her life, but she wasn't going to feel sorry for herself either. She would take advantage of this time to figure things out and somehow get her life back to normal.

With determination for a better life echoing through her mind, she raised her head and looked out the window beyond her campsite. Wyatt walked by at the same moment and glanced into her trailer window with a smile. He lifted a hand in a small wave, and Aubree did the same. Then she leaned her head back against the wood paneling and tried to calm her racing heart.

EIGHTEEN

* * *

AUBREE DIDN'T DRIFT OFF to sleep until it was nearly midnight. Her brain buzzed with thoughts of Tidmore, Jason, and the people chasing her. She had a halfhearted notion that she could stay hidden in these mountains forever and not be found. She pulled closer to Scarlett and listened to her rhythmic breathing. If only there were a way to put an end to all the chaos and danger pursuing her.

By morning, Aubree's thoughts had turned to the day she'd left Omaha nearly two weeks before. She sat at the tiny kitchen table and held a mug of steaming hot cocoa in her hands. The television screen with Governor Brent Ferrin flashed through her mind, and she kept hearing that familiar voice and getting cold chills. The memories flitted through her mind, and she tried to grasp the idea that had come to her. Maybe her memory of the conversation really did hold the key to unlocking the mystery. She wished there were some way to escape the nameless, faceless voice that had uprooted her life. There was something in the back of her mind. It felt like having a word on the tip of her tongue, but instead it was some piece of information locked in her memory—if she could just retrieve it, Aubree felt it would fit into the puzzle of the crime.

Scarlett began to fuss and roll around on the bed, and Aubree smiled, glad for the diversion. "It's good I have you to worry about, or I might go crazy." She kissed Scarlett's soft cheeks and held her close. "Let's get you some breakfast, and then we'll go for a walk."

Scarlett was a good eater, and while Aubree fed her, she mentally took inventory of her food storage. In about ten days, she'd have to leave the campground for more food and supplies. Her stomach tightened with dread at the prospect of leaving her safe haven. Then it tightened again as she looked down a road with no future. As long as her enemies were after her, they held her future hostage.

Aubree hurried to dress Scarlett and walked out into the sunshine, leaving her worries behind for a moment. She'd fallen into a bit of a routine, which included a walk each morning before Scarlett's first nap. They had made it halfway around the circle of campsites when she heard footsteps behind her. She glanced over her shoulder, and her heart lurched when she recognized Wyatt in his park ranger uniform.

"Good morning, Aubree." He quickened his pace to close the last few steps between them. "Are you out for a stroll?"

"Every day. This campground is really beautiful," Aubree said, and she mentally scolded herself for the butterflies in her stomach.

"It is. It's kind of an out-of-the-way place—makes me wonder why people decide to come here when the beaches of Bear Lake are beckoning from only twenty miles out." He stared at her for a moment, and Aubree wondered again if she should trust him.

"Hmm, that's probably why," she replied. "Bear Lake is pretty busy— lots of tourists." She continued walking.

"And it gets busier every year, it seems." He walked casually alongside her. "But we stay pretty busy here, too, for such a small place." He stooped to pick up a piece of trash, and Aubree could see the dark tan across the back of his neck.

"Are you outside all day?"

"Pretty much." Wyatt grinned. "I love it. How about you? Do you camp here often?"

"Uh, it's been a long time since I've been camping." Aubree's palms felt hot. She hadn't anticipated answering so many questions. "I decided to bring Scarlett and take a break from everything. It's been a stressful year."

Wyatt paused, seeming to take in the full meaning of her statement. "It must be hard losing your husband. I'm glad God created mountains so we could get away from everything."

Tears gathered in the corners of her eyes, and Aubree bent over, pretending to check something on Scarlett's stroller.

"I know it's not the same, but I lost a little brother last year." Wyatt tugged on a curl near the nape of his neck. "He was killed by a drunk driver on his way up Logan Canyon." The hollow spot on his throat tensed, and he frowned. "I still think about him every day and wonder how things could be different."

Aubree wiped her hand across her eyes and pushed the stroller forward. "There've been a few days when I haven't thought about my husband, and I've felt guilty for that, but I know he wouldn't want me to."

"Yeah, the guilt almost drove me over the edge at first," Wyatt said softly.

"Guilt? But why?" Aubree looked at him carefully.

"Carson was coming to see me." Wyatt kicked at a rock lodged in the dirt road. "If I hadn't been here, he would still be alive."

"But it's my fault too—that my husband was killed. All because of a wrong number."

Wyatt's head snapped up, and Aubree gripped the curved handles of the umbrella stroller with white knuckles. "I mean—"

"No, you don't have to explain. I'm sorry. I always ask too many questions."

Aubree swallowed. "It's okay. It's just hard to talk about."

He nodded. "But I hope you can stop blaming yourself." Wyatt's eyes softened, and he frowned. "I couldn't at first, and then I had a dream. Carson told me it was okay, and he told me he was happy. He—" Wyatt swallowed and gave Aubree a crooked smile. "I haven't told anyone outside my family about this, but Carson—he told me he loved me and that I should open my heart to the future."

A tear trickled down Aubree's cheek. "That's beautiful. I wish I could find the same peace."

"I hope you can too. I hope the sadness doesn't haunt you."

"That's just it. Something *is* haunting me and no matter how hard I run I can't escape," Aubree said. "But I shouldn't even be bringing it up. I'm sorry."

They had walked almost the entire loop of the campground, and her trailer was back in sight. "I should be going now."

"Wait." Wyatt reached out and touched her arm. "Please, I didn't mean to unload on you. I'm sorry."

"No, it's not that." Aubree could feel her cheeks growing warm again. "It's just that I'm kind of in a mess right now."

"I wish I could help you," Wyatt said.

"No one can help me. I'd better go." Aubree pushed the stroller as fast as she could. Scarlett giggled and squealed as the wheels bumped along the ground. When she turned to get Scarlett out of the stroller, she saw Wyatt still standing in the middle of the road. His brow was furrowed, and he had his hands in his pockets. A few locks of his dark brown hair caught the glint of the sun. He held up his hand as if to wave and then turned around and walked back up the road.

Aubree's hands shook as she sat with Scarlett on the bed in the trailer. She hummed a melody and rocked her gently, trying not to let her tears fall onto the dark curls of her baby's head. Loneliness hadn't caught up to her lately, and her shoulders shook with new sobs as she replayed her words: *No one can help me.*

She thought about what Wyatt had mentioned—the guilty feelings and how he didn't blame himself anymore, and she wondered if she would ever be able to say that about Devin's death. She hadn't meant to speak about how she felt responsible for his death. The words popped out of her mouth before she could stop them. She'd let her guard down. It had been a risky move, but it felt good. To finally be able to share her true feelings with someone for even a short time had lifted a weight from her shoulders.

"We can't live like this forever, Scarlett. I've got to find a way to get our life back," Aubree whispered as she stroked the porcelain cheek of her baby girl.

NINETEEN

* * *

WYATT HAD LOOKED so forlorn and disappointed the day before that Aubree was shocked when he showed up during her morning walk the next day.

"Hey, I wanted to say I'm sorry about yesterday." He twirled his park ranger hat on one finger. "I didn't mean to get so personal."

"Oh, me too," Aubree agreed.

"I guess it's just tough stuff to talk about, huh?" Wyatt gave her a bright smile. "So how about we talk about something different today?"

Aubree hesitated before shrugging. "Sounds like a deal."

They spent the next hour talking about their favorite movies and music. It was lighthearted conversation, and Aubree felt reckless, conversing as if she had nothing to hide.

Wyatt walked close to her and even pushed Scarlett's stroller for a while. By the time they finished walking, the heat had made Aubree's neck sticky with sweat. Scarlett had fallen asleep, and her head rested at an awkward angle.

"I'm sorry I kept you so long," Wyatt said.

Aubree smiled. "I could say the same thing." During their walk, Aubree had wondered if it was dangerous talking to a stranger. But Wyatt didn't seem like a stranger. It felt so good to have someone listen to her, even if the conversation centered on media and entertainment.

The next morning, Aubree told herself it would be okay to talk to someone besides Scarlett once in a while, and she found herself looking for Wyatt. He didn't disappoint, and he talked her ear off all around the campground.

A week passed, and Aubree visited with Wyatt a little bit longer each day. She tried to keep her defenses up, but he was slowly chipping away at her barrier.

"I'd really like to get to know the real Aubree," he said one day after they had walked around the loop of the campground three times. They stood in the shade of a pine tree, and Aubree watched a chipmunk scamper through the pine needles on the forest floor.

"This is the real me," she said.

"You know what I mean." He touched her chin and looked into her eyes. "Something has you scared enough that you've closed off a part of you. I'm not going to hurt you. I just want to know you."

Aubree stepped back and shrugged. "I guess I'm a little shy."

Wyatt's lips twitched as if he were about to say more, then he shook his head. "Maybe I'll see you tomorrow?"

Aubree smiled. "Sure."

✳ ✳ ✳

"Agent Edwards, I need you in L.A., not roaming the countryside checking out campgrounds," Agent Napierski spoke forcefully, and Jason held the phone away from his ear. Jason had been arguing with his supervisor since he set out on Aubree's trail a week and a half ago. "She had a full tank of gas when she left Aurora, and I'm almost certain she was heading west. I think she's trying to get closer to her mom. Just give me a couple more days. I'll find her."

"I'm sorry, but I need your neurons firing on the information that just came in on this case. Leave the searching to Stokes and his team. They'll find her." Agent Napierski's tone didn't leave any room for argument.

"Sir, could you give me forty-eight hours? The enemy may already have someone in place."

"Edwards, I want you in this office tomorrow morning," Napierski barked.

"Yes, sir," Jason said. He clenched his phone in one hand and squeezed the bridge of his nose with the other. If someone got to Aubree before him, would she be able to recognize the danger?

✳ ✳ ✳

It had been almost two weeks, and Wyatt always seemed to show up when Aubree and Scarlett ventured outside. On day seventeen of Aubree's stay in the Paris Springs Campground, Wyatt surprised her with a question. "Would you like to go fishing sometime?"

"I'm not very good at it," she said. "But I'd like to try again. It's been a long time."

His smile widened into a boyish grin, and she couldn't help smiling back.

"How about tomorrow? I can pick you up after I do my rounds."

She lowered her eyes. "Okay."

The next morning, Aubree experienced some nervous jitters as she packed a lunch and got Scarlett ready. Her heart jumped when she heard a light knock on the door. She smiled at her nervousness and took a deep breath before answering the door. "Good morning, Wyatt."

He grinned, and the smile crinkled the skin around his eyes. "Good mornin' to you too. Can I hold Scarlett?"

Scarlett giggled when Wyatt blew a raspberry on her hand and kept squealing all the way to his pickup. Aubree felt her nerves relaxing a bit once they were on their way.

"Now, there's one nice thing about fishing with a park ranger." Wyatt grinned and tapped his steering wheel to the country music on his radio. "We can park wherever we want and fish as long as we like."

The lake was beautiful and secluded. Every so often, she could see small ripples of movement where a fish brushed the top of the tranquil water and broke the stillness. Wild grasses poked up between the rocks hugging the shoreline of the lake. As they walked, the dust billowed up in thick clouds along the trail, and by the time Wyatt found the fishing spot he was looking for, Aubree's socks were covered with dirt. She hefted Scarlett higher on her hip and pointed out the sun above the line of pine trees in the distance.

"See the sun? It's smiling at you," she told Scarlett. The baby waved chubby hands at the sky and jabbered something excitedly.

Wyatt shaded his eyes and surveyed the area. He frowned for a second and seemed to be deep in thought. He lifted his eyes to meet Aubree's and chuckled, then reached for Scarlett. "Do you want to see some fish?"

Scarlett clutched him happily as she continued to babble. Wyatt's cheeks reddened with pleasure, and Aubree couldn't help but smile. She tried to ignore the twinge of pain reminding her that it should be Devin holding this child. She pushed her hair behind her ears and felt the sun on her face. She would enjoy one day without guilt. Maybe.

Wyatt had his line baited in no time, and Aubree was surprised he didn't use a worm. "What's that?"

"It's rainbow colored power bait, to attract the fish." He pointed at a small jar filled with yellow and green goo that had orange stripes running through it. "It works ten times better than a worm."

Aubree remembered going fishing with her father and trying to hold the squiggly worm for him to put on the hook. "That looks easier than using a worm anyway," she said.

"Yeah, here you go. Would you like to be the first to cast out?"

"I don't think I can. I'll just watch you."

"All right, but next cast you have to try," Wyatt said. He stood and lifted the pole out to his side. "It's really not too hard, you just press this trigger and pretend you're like a big clock, and when your arm hits one o'clock, you release and boom! There she goes."

His arm reached out gracefully over the lake, and Aubree watched as the line disappeared somewhere in the water about a hundred feet away.

"I'll never be able to do that," she said.

"Sure you will, it'll come back to you." Wyatt set his pole against a rock. He picked up a heavy blanket and spread it on the ground. "You can sit over here with Scarlett if you want."

"Thanks." Aubree walked over to the edge of the blanket and sat down. Scarlett pointed and giggled as she crawled around the blanket. Wyatt handed the baby a pinecone.

"Now don't eat it, little chipmunk." He squeezed her chubby cheeks.

Scarlett laughed, then patted her cheeks and smacked her lips together as if she were giving Wyatt a kiss. He leaned over to kiss her cheek and made a growling noise. Scarlett screeched, and Aubree couldn't help herself. She laughed with them.

About five minutes later, Aubree jumped up, pointing at the fishing pole. "It moved! I saw it move!"

"Hey, maybe we've got one." Wyatt clapped his hands. "Do you remember what to do next?"

"Umm, reel it in?" Aubree asked.

"Come here." Wyatt took her hands and put them around the pole. "First you have to pull up fast so the hook will catch on the fish. Like this." He lifted her hands up, and the pole jerked back.

Aubree squealed, and Wyatt chuckled in her ear. "Now go ahead and reel that baby in." He moved a lever on the reel and put Aubree's hand on the crank to get her started. Then he stepped back and picked Scarlett up to watch. Aubree could feel a definite pull on the line as she reeled it in. She looked hesitantly at Wyatt and then grinned at Scarlett. "We caught a fish! Here he comes."

She could see the speckled trout fighting in the water as she pulled it closer to shore. "Now what do I do?" Aubree asked, shrieking as the fish jumped and splashed in the water.

Wyatt held out his fishing net. "Grab hold of the line and drop him in."

Aubree shied away from the wiggling fish but was finally able to get him in the net.

"Now how about we trade? You can put the pole down, and I'll take it from here." He grinned and held out Scarlett, who was watching the fish with wide eyes.

"Did you see Mommy catch a fish?" Aubree held Scarlett close and pointed at the wriggling trout.

Scarlett reached out and patted Aubree's cheek. "Ma, ma, ma."

"Yes, Mama did it!"

"Hey, how long has she been saying your name?" Wyatt asked as he cleaned the fish.

"Oh, she's just babbling. But it sounds like she says all kinds of gibberish."

"I bet you love to hear her pretty little voice every day." Wyatt winked at Scarlett.

"I do." Aubree kissed Scarlett's cheek and sat on the blanket with her.

"You're a good mom," Wyatt said. "Now how about we try this again?"

Aubree's throat tingled as she absorbed the compliment. "Thanks. That means a lot." She brushed off her pants and stood up. "I guess since you're being so nice that means I have to try casting, huh?"

"Hey, I'm always nice. But, yes, it's your turn." Wyatt grinned and held up the fishing pole.

It took several tries, but Aubree finally got a good line out. She tried to ignore the fluttering in her stomach when Wyatt took her hands and guided her arms to cast the line. They were enjoying the calm atmosphere of the lake, and Aubree kept telling herself to relax, but she watched Wyatt closely. Several times, she noticed him surveying the area and chewing on the inside of his cheek. Finally she asked, "What are you looking for?"

"That's just it—I don't know. I'm following your lead."

Aubree furrowed her brow. "My lead?"

"Yeah. Every few minutes you're looking over your shoulder like you're expecting to see someone." He glanced around the lake again. "I'm just wondering who you're waiting for." His eyes flickered and then focused on her face.

Aubree froze and tension arced through her body. Of course. She was always aware of her surroundings, always checking out every person in proximity, but she didn't want Wyatt to know why. She gulped. "Nobody—I just haven't ever been able to . . . ." She pulled her shoe through the filmy dirt. "It's paranoia. You know, panic attacks and stuff since my husband died."

Wyatt groaned and covered his face with a hand. "Man, I was way out of line. I'm really sorry."

"It's okay." Aubree shrugged. "Don't worry about it."

He shook his head. "But I am worried about it. You're hard to read, and I don't want to make you uncomfortable."

With a smile, Aubree waved her hand. "It's okay. I'm having a great time today."

"Are you sure?"

"Yes. Let's catch some more fish."

Even with the questions flowing on a current of anxiety through her mind, she still felt attracted to Wyatt. It was foolish, and she knew it, but she couldn't ignore how she felt and how much Scarlett adored him.

It was a first for her baby. Scarlett had never been around anyone else. But despite that, she couldn't get enough of Wyatt. Aubree kept telling herself not to get too comfortable, not to trust, and not to let her guard down. But she wasn't listening to herself very well.

After a successful day of fishing and a delicious fish fry, courtesy of Wyatt's culinary skills, Aubree was exhausted. Scarlett slept in the trailer, and Aubree sat next to Wyatt in some old lawn chairs near the crackling fire. He reached out and took her hand. "Thanks for coming with me today. I haven't had that much fun in a long time."

At first, Aubree thought about withdrawing her hand. But then Wyatt gave her one of his stellar grins and squeezed her fingers, and she shrugged mentally.

"You're a good guy, aren't you, Wyatt Erickson?"

"I hope you think so."

"Thanks for taking me fishing. It was the best time I've had in—well, I guess it's been too long." Aubree stared at the fire and tried to think of a time during the last year when she'd been this relaxed. She squinted at the dancing flames, knowing there hadn't been any.

"I guess you're getting close to three weeks at this campsite. How long are you planning on staying?" Wyatt asked.

Aubree tensed and wished she had an answer for that question. "To be honest, I don't really know." She pursed her lips and listened to the wood popping in the fire. "I guess I'm getting low on supplies, but hopefully I'll stay a bit longer."

"I hope so, too." Wyatt leaned toward her, and his eyes looked brown in the darkness falling around them. Aubree was suddenly aware of every heartbeat, and she looked down at their hands clasped together. Unbidden, the memory of the voice came to mind. She could see herself running out of the house in Omaha and driving for her life, with Scarlett sleeping in the car seat. Her palms began to sweat, and she released Wyatt's hand.

"It's getting late, and I need to check Scarlett. It's been a while since she's had a diaper change, and she'll probably be waking up soon." She knew she was babbling, but she couldn't make herself stop. "Thanks again for the wonderful day." She stood and turned to walk into the trailer, but Wyatt was out of his chair in an instant. He stepped in front of her.

"Wait. I did it again, didn't I?" He rubbed his forehead with his hand and gazed down at her. "Don't go. I don't want you to go."

Aubree swallowed hard. "I'm just—it's getting late. I'll still be here in the morning." She tried to laugh, but it lodged in her throat when Wyatt reached forward and pulled her into his arms.

"Aubree, everytime I feel like I'm one step closer to getting to know you, you do the hundred yard dash and leave me in the dust."

Her body was rigid in his arms, and a thousand thoughts buzzed through her mind. She tried to think what she should do. She thought about her FBI training and the witness protection program and about all the times she had distanced herself from her neighbors in Omaha.

Wyatt rubbed her back and leaned closer to her. "I know there must be a reason, but I can't stop chasing you. Would it be that bad if I caught up to you just once?"

A lump of emotion rose in Aubree's throat, and when she tried to speak, all that came out was a gurgling, "I don't know."

"I want to invite you to come down to Logan with me and meet my family. They could vouch for me." He leaned back and smiled at her, but she could see all the emotions playing behind his eyes.

"I can't. I can't do that to you. I won't hurt you, Wyatt." She moved quickly—out of his arms and into the trailer. "I'm sorry," she whispered and shut the door. She barely made it to the back of the trailer before a cry escaped from her throat. Scarlett was still asleep, so Aubree curled up in a ball and tried not to wake her as she sobbed into the blanket.

Tears of rage, disappointment, and fear poured out. Why did this have to happen to her? Why did Scarlett have to be born without a father and live on the run with her helpless mother?

She thought about Wyatt and shook her head angrily. There was no choice; she'd have to leave in the morning. She couldn't risk hurting him—hurting someone else because of the mess she was in. A fresh surge of tears tore at her throat as she thought about Wyatt's arms around her. She'd wanted so much to stay there and let him hold her. If only he could make everything right in her world again.

Aubree didn't know how long she cried, but her throat was dry, and her eyes were sore, so she stood to get a glass of water. She drank the freezing water and splashed her face in the enamel sink. It was dark outside, but she never had any idea what time it was in the mountains. She turned and held her watch up to the glow of the firelight outside. The watch indicated it was past ten o'clock. When she looked out the window, she caught her breath.

A figure sat in a chair beside the fire with his head in his hands. Wyatt was still there. Before she could move, he lifted his head as if he felt her watching him. He stood and moved toward her until he was standing right by the window.

"Aubree," he whispered. "Can I please come in and talk to you for a minute? Or will you come out here?"

"I'm sorry." She pulled the faded curtains closed. There was silence for a few seconds, and then she heard the crunch of boots on the dirt path.

TWENTY

✳ ✳ ✳

WHEN SCARLETT WOKE THE next morning, Aubree fed her and then lay back down on the bed to close her eyes. She felt horrible. Her eyes were swollen from crying, and her mind had run a marathon of thoughts all night as she continually mulled over her options.

The guide to campsites around the area showed several different choices, but Aubree wondered if they would be as remote as Paris Springs. Part of her wanted to leave to keep from hurting Wyatt and to ensure Scarlett's safety, and another part wanted to stay. After sorting through her notes of the case and her scribbled transcripts of the conversation, Aubree felt sure there was still something in her memory that held the key to her case. But with the confused state of mind she was in, she might never be able to extract the detail that hovered on the edges of all her dreams.

Even though she wanted to skip their morning walk, Scarlett was fussy, and Aubree knew she needed to talk to Wyatt. Although it was later than usual when they strolled around the campground, Wyatt wasn't there. She listened for the familiar *clomp, clomp* of his boots and glanced over her shoulder several times as they made the loop of the campground, but he didn't come.

The day felt hotter than usual, and Aubree's heart was heavy. "I ruined a good thing, but I guess it's for the best," she told Scarlett. She concentrated her energy on cleaning up the camp trailer and making a list of supplies they would need to move to another campground. Biting her lip, she told herself not to cry and to remember that if she really cared about Wyatt, she wouldn't put him in danger.

She found herself looking out the window when someone walked by and jumping at every sound, hoping it was Wyatt's vehicle. But she didn't see him. Her head ached as she worried over whether she'd made the right choice in pushing him away. She put her head in her hands and thought, *I'll leave tomorrow before there's a chance of running into him again.*

At ten o'clock the next day, instead of going for a stroll, Aubree walked around her trailer removing the rocks that had held it steady for the past three weeks. When she came around the back end of the trailer, she stooped to retrieve the rock and groaned.

"A flat tire!" Her eyes stung with frustration, and she stomped back into the trailer. She dug around and found a jack, but it was different from a car jack, and she'd never changed a tire on her own before.

Taking the jack outside, she examined the tire and began loosening the lug nuts with the tire wrench. She twisted as hard as she could until she heard a pop and a crack and the wrench fell off. The twisted metal of a broken lug nut lay on the ground. Aubree sat in the dirt with her head in her hands. She would have to find someone to help her change the tire, but that would mean talking to someone she didn't trust. Scarlett fussed inside the trailer, and Aubree went back inside to feed her.

"I guess we'll have to put off leaving until I can figure out what to do about that tire," Aubree told Scarlett as she stroked her hair.

When Scarlett fell asleep, Aubree busied herself with organizing the dishes in the cupboard. *Maybe I'll be able to ask the camp chief for help when he comes to gather payments today.* Perhaps she should try to ask someone else in the campground for help, but part of her wanted to stay at Paris Springs. That part had her continually looking down the road for a sign of a familiar park ranger.

As the day turned to dusk and there was still no sign of Wyatt or the camp chief, Aubree decided to light one last fire. In the morning, she would take courage and ask someone to help her with the trailer. When the fire crackled brightly, Aubree returned to the trailer to feed Scarlett some dinner. Afterwards, they sat by the fire, and Scarlett snuggled into Aubree's chest. Rocking her baby from side to side, Aubree sang to her softly until Scarlett's dark lashes drooped into a deep sleep.

Aubree walked carefully with her sleeping bundle and climbed into the trailer. It felt a bit chilly, so she tucked a few extra blankets around

Scarlett, turned off the lights, and sat at the kitchen table in the dark, gazing out the window. The night was black, and the fire popped intermittently, sending red sparks into the air. Gravel crunched under a heavy footstep outside her trailer, and Aubree's ears strained for sound. Someone walked around the side of her trailer and approached the fire. Squinting through the darkness, Aubree felt her heart in her throat when she saw the silhouette of a man by the fire.

It was Wyatt. He poked around the fire and glanced toward the trailer. He must've figured she was inside, but he couldn't see her in the dark. A couple of times he took a few steps toward her door and then turned back. She watched him sit on a log near the fire and lean his elbows on his knees.

He was still there even though she'd turned him away. Aubree closed her eyes and took a deep breath, the inner turmoil she'd been fighting the past two days rose to the surface. She heard a sound and opened her eyes. Wyatt took a few steps toward the trailer and then hesitated. He looked up to the sky and rubbed a hand back and forth over his jaw.

Aubree stood and felt the strands of her short hair, trying to remember what color it was, where she was, who she was. She clenched her teeth together and stepped toward the door. She thrust it open and stared down at Wyatt.

"My name is Aubree Stewart. I have strawberry-blonde hair, blue eyes, and a year ago I lived in San Diego, California. I was unlucky enough to overhear details about the plot to kill the secretary of defense, and my husband was murdered because of it. I was in the witness protection program, but even that failed me. I can't see you anymore because I don't want you to get hurt too."

The chilly mountain air hung between them, and for a moment everything was quiet. Then Wyatt cleared his throat.

"And what if I won't take no for an answer? What if I'm willing to risk my life just to know you?"

It was the last thing Aubree had expected to hear. She stumbled backwards and slumped into the cushions surrounding the dinette table. Wyatt stopped the door before it swung shut and stepped into the trailer.

He sat across from her at the table and spoke in a low voice. "For the past two days, I've been thinking, trying to figure you out, and hoping for a chance to talk to you." He leaned forward and clasped his hands behind his neck. "I decided it didn't matter what happened to you or what you did or didn't do—I want to know you. Please tell me anything, everything—whatever you can."

She stared at him for a few seconds and then glanced back at the sleeping lump Scarlett made on the bed. "I was going to leave today, but the trailer has a flat tire."

Wyatt grinned. "Whoever said flat tires were a bad thing?" Then his face grew serious. "Please don't leave. At least give me a chance to help you."

She took a deep breath, pausing before she told Wyatt the craziest story anyone could think up—except that it was true. It was the first time she'd unloaded every detail, even those she'd kept from her mother. Wyatt sat still and listened.

After nearly an hour of talking, Aubree stopped and got up for a glass of water. She offered one to Wyatt and then sat again. "So I've stayed away from everyone and tried to play the role set up for me, but I can't get away from the memories.

"Whenever I get feeling down, I start thinking about Devin again. Even though part of me still feels betrayed and angry with him, I wish I could be with him—that maybe if we spent time together I'd feel better somehow." Aubree turned and looked out the window.

Wyatt kept quiet, staring at her and listening intently. She spread her hands out on the chipped Formica tabletop. "But I can't. I can't be with him anymore. Even though I'd love to feel his arms around me, to lay my head against his shoulder, and to just breathe there and feel safe, I'm not safe. Nothing is safe anymore."

Wyatt winced and blew out his breath. "I didn't know. I don't know what to say. I feel like a fool."

"No, please don't feel that way. The past few weeks have been great. I can almost forget sometimes that I'm hiding—running for my life out here. But I can't live like this forever. I've got to figure something out."

"Let me help you." Wyatt reached for her hand.

Aubree hesitated and then clasped his strong, warm hand. The fire glowed red and cast a dim light on the interior of the trailer. She looked at Wyatt and at their hands clasped together. His eyes were focused on hers. The trees outside scraped against the side of the trailer as a gust of wind blew through the campground. The rushing of the creek was like a soft padding against the night noises, and Aubree wished the soothing noise could fill her mind and overpower the millions of disjointed thoughts running through her head.

Wyatt pulled her hand to his mouth and kissed it. The kiss left a shimmery spot of wetness against her fingers, and Aubree breathed deeply. She could smell the campfire and Wyatt's scent of clean aftershave mixed with pine, willows, and freshly chopped wood. He smelled good, like all the places he'd been that day, and as Aubree stared at him, she wanted to believe that he was good—that he was someone she could trust—and so she continued, "What hurts the most and keeps me up at night—what tears my heart right out—is to think that if something happened to me, if I died, then this sweet baby wouldn't even remember me." She pointed at Scarlett.

"She's my whole life, and I've given everything for her, but she wouldn't even remember me if I was gone." Aubree squeezed her eyes shut. "I've got to be here for her. This world is so scary. She needs me, but I don't know what will happen."

Wyatt put his other hand on top of hers. "I'm so sorry you've had to carry this by yourself. But you've done a good job. Scarlett is a happy, beautiful baby."

Aubree glanced at Scarlett and whispered. "I look at her chubby cheeks and blue eyes, and it makes me want to cry because I think of how she smiles at me and how she laughs when I kiss her." Her voice grew husky with more tears, but she continued talking anyway. "I think of how Scarlett loves me so much and how I love her more than I thought I could love anything, but how long would it take her to forget me?"

"Nothing's going to happen to you, Aubree. You'll be there for her when she goes to kindergarten and when she graduates from high school. You'll be there."

Aubree stood up. "But you don't know that!" Her voice was a strangled cry. "Maybe I'll outrun them until she goes to kindergarten and then something will happen to me. How much do you remember from when you were five years old?" She wiped her eyes and clenched her teeth. "I don't want her to forget how much I love her. And the only way she's going to remember is if I'm here every day of her life to tell her, to take care of her, and to show her."

Wyatt slid from behind the table to stand next to her. "You're gonna make it," he whispered softly. "We'll outsmart these guys. We'll find out who they are and what they're up to." He pulled her into a fierce hug. "It's gonna be okay."

This time, Aubree let him hold her. She let her tears fall onto his shirt and breathed in the woodsy scent of this park ranger who had found her and broken down all of her defenses.

He held her close and kissed the top of her head. "You need someone you can trust, and I'm right here for you."

Scarlett stirred and Aubree went to tuck the blankets around her. Wyatt watched and whispered, "Can we go outside and talk? I have about a million questions for you."

Aubree smiled through her tears, and when he reached for her hand, she took it and let him lead her outside. Later that evening, after Wyatt had wished her good night, Aubree sat beside the dying embers of the fire. The stars twinkled through the canopy of pine trees overhead, and Aubree inhaled deeply, trying to clear her mind.

She pushed back the fear that she had made a mistake in confiding in Wyatt. She had to trust him. She'd just unloaded her soul to him, and he was willing to help her. Thinking of Devin, she shook her head. Was it a betrayal to him that she had feelings for Wyatt? Could she let someone else into her heart? Aubree ran her fingers through her hair and sighed. She didn't want to think about a relationship right now. She needed to figure out how she and Scarlett could stay alive.

After talking with Wyatt, she felt even more strongly than before that there was a way for her to get out of this mess. Evidently, the people who had killed Devin believed there was a lot to the conversation she'd heard on the cell phone. And now, almost a year later, they were still after her because she had something tucked away in the recesses of her mind that could stop them—hurt them even. Her skin tingled, and her breath hung in mists around her. She looked up again at the midnight sky and whispered, "Help me find a way. Help me to know how I can keep Scarlett safe."

TWENTY-ONE

✳ ✳ ✳

T HE NEXT MORNING, AUBREE woke feeling different. She cuddled
next to Scarlett and thought about the light feeling in her heart.
Even though she knew someone was still out there somewhere, hunting her down, she felt safer because Wyatt knew her story. And he said
he would help her. Maybe together they could find a way to end the
chase.

After a quick breakfast of cereal with powdered milk, Aubree pulled
out a notebook and started jotting things down. She made a plan to find
the nearest Internet access and do a bit of research. She had always relied
on Jason to ask all the questions about her case and trusted the FBI to
research and find the answers, but now she was on her own.

She re-read all of the notes she'd taken and analyzed a few of the
sentences. Several versions of the conversation were scrawled throughout a tattered notebook. Her mind buzzed with new energy. Unloading
everything to Wyatt had awakened some of the details of her case, and
it was as if she were looking at things for the first time. She read through
her makeshift transcripts.

"*Tidmore did the job, and the body is hidden in the manhole on 32nd
Street like we talked about.*" Her memory wasn't clear on the next part
of the conversation. She knew he had said something about when they
found the body, they'd be in the green. And then she was certain he'd
said, "*The intruder will clear the way.*"—and then the words that uncovered the identity of his victim: "*Hey, don't I at least get a congrats? What's
up with you? I even kept his uniform for you.*"

Massaging her forehead, Aubree hoped something in the words might spark a fragment of memory in her brain or somehow connect the information the murderer thought she had. Apparently, she'd heard enough in that phone call for someone to want her dead. Why couldn't she piece together what it was? Was it just the voice or something more?

Scarlett screeched at her and waved her hands, and Aubree noticed it was already past eleven o'clock. "Oops, I guess we're late for our walk this morning, aren't we?" She smiled at Scarlett and stretched. The baby reached her arms up too. They had both slept late, and Aubree wondered if they would miss Wyatt this morning because they were off their usual schedule. Then she laughed at herself. They were staying in a remote camping area in Idaho, hiding out, and she still had a schedule.

Aubree pushed the stroller about halfway around the campground before she heard the familiar *clomp, clomp* of Wyatt's boots behind her. She turned around and shaded her eyes with her hand. "Long time, no see."

He chuckled. "I was wondering if I had missed your morning stroll. I'm sorry I've missed it the past couple days." He bent over and ruffled the curls on Scarlett's head. "Someone kept me up way past my bedtime last night." He grinned and raised his eyebrows at Aubree. "So I decided we would all probably need a pick-me-up for lunch, so I picked up lunch." He smiled at his play on words and lifted a brown paper sack with grease spots. Aubree caught the unmistakable whiff of French fries, and her mouth watered.

"Hometown Drive-In makes the best burgers and fries around here—oh shucks. I forgot that I have a fresh raspberry shake in the cooler in my truck." He tilted his head towards the parking area where he left his pickup.

"Well, I definitely wouldn't mind going to help you get it."

"Good. Let's keep walking then, shall we, Miss Scarlett?"

Aubree watched him interacting with her baby and felt her heart tugging with those familiar strings of regret for Devin, but she shook her head and ordered herself to look to the future. She reached for Wyatt's hand, and his smile widened until the skin around his eyes crinkled. Then he interlaced his fingers with hers.

"Wyatt, don't park rangers usually stay busier than you?"

His cheeks flushed, and he grinned. "Well, actually, I've been putting in some odd hours lately so I have more time during the day."

"What kind of odd hours?"

"Starting my rounds at 4 a.m." He stretched his arms above his head. "So I'm usually finished with most of my duties before lunchtime, and then I can always go back out later too."

"But why?"

"So I could spend more time with you and Scarlett."

Now it was Aubree's turn to blush. Wyatt was always open and honest. She felt like he didn't keep any secrets from her. Secrets—of course that topic brought a twinge of pain to her heart.

"Are you okay? Maybe I shouldn't have told you." He looked worried.

"No, that's just it. I'm so glad you did tell me, and it means a lot that you would do that for us—that you would worry so much about us."

"I worry about you, but that's not the only reason I've rearranged my schedule. I need to see you every day. The day's not right if I don't see you and Scarlett."

He stopped walking and pulled her in close to him. Her awareness of his closeness made her neck flush with heat, and she rested her head on his shoulder.

"I want to keep seeing you and Scarlett. I really care about you both. These past few weeks have been—" he swallowed and held her tighter. "They've been what I've looked for my whole life."

Aubree looked up at him and smiled. He grinned back and leaned closer to her. "I want to help you find your freedom again, so I can enjoy it with you."

She didn't want to cry in front of him, but she felt moisture on her cheeks again and blinked her eyes to clear them of tears. She didn't understand why Wyatt would want her, a widowed woman with a baby. But right now, she wasn't going to analyze it. She could enjoy the warmth of his arms around her. Later she would decide what to do. "Thank you," she murmured.

"My pleasure." Wyatt chuckled and pulled his head back. He stared at her for a second, and Aubree felt her pulse beating in her neck. He smiled, and she noticed a few freckles on his cheeks. The muscles in his arms felt solid as he pulled her closer. She leaned into him, and he brought his face closer to hers, all the time looking into her eyes.

She closed her eyes and felt the warmth of his breath on her lips as he kissed her gently. Aubree surprised herself by kissing him back and wrapping her arms around his neck before she regained her senses and pulled away. Wyatt laughed and pulled her back to him in a tight embrace. Scarlett squealed in the stroller and clapped her hands. "See? She's happy about this idea too," Wyatt said.

Aubree leaned down and patted Scarlett's cheek. "Well, as long as I have your permission." She turned and winked at Wyatt and took a deep breath to calm her fluttering heart. "I've been thinking all morning about the murder and the bits and pieces I know about it. I need access to the Internet to look some things up."

"If we go in closer to Bear Lake, there's a place with a couple computers they let people pay to use."

Aubree pointed at Scarlett. "We're down to the last of her diapers. I hadn't planned on staying put for quite so long."

"Do you mind if I come along as your tour guide?" Wyatt tapped his hat. "A park ranger can be a handy thing to have around."

"I think that sounds like a good idea." Aubree stepped closer to him. "Can I schedule my guided tour for tomorrow? I need some more time to gather my thoughts today."

Wyatt put his arm around her, pulling her into his chest. He leaned in for one more kiss, and Aubree's heart raced as his lips met hers. Her lips warmed to his touch, and they kissed several times before she leaned her head against his chest.

Wyatt rubbed her back, and she listened to his heart thrum through the soft cotton of his shirt as she enjoyed the tingling feeling in her lips.

"Listen, I know you've been worried about venturing outside of the campground by yourself, so I want to show you something that's only a few miles away—a wonderful scenic attraction I'm sure you've missed." He reached one of his bronzed arms out and pointed west of the camping area. "The ice cave."

"Ice cave?" Aubree raised her eyebrows. "You're serious?"

Wyatt laughed. "Of course I'm serious. It's pretty neat, and I want to take you and Scarlett to a place where there's snow year round."

"But it's almost August. How could there be snow down here?"

"I'll show you after lunch." Wyatt released Aubree and took charge of pushing Scarlett's stroller. She watched him for half a second, taking in his tanned skin and dark, wavy hair. It was nice to have something pleasant to distract her thoughts. It wasn't as if she hadn't noticed how good-looking Wyatt was before, but she hadn't really let herself look because she was too busy holding up her shield of defense. Trust was an amazing thing. It was like someone had wiped the film off her window, and she could finally look at the world and enjoy it—almost without fear. When she was with Wyatt, she wasn't afraid that someone would find her. Aubree touched her lips, smiled, and then hurried to keep up with Wyatt's long strides.

A couple miles from the Paris Springs Campground down a dusty dirt road, they saw the scenic attraction called the Ice Cave. Aubree was less than impressed when she climbed out of Wyatt's pickup and looked at the face of a rocky hill covered with ugly dying weeds and brown grasses.

"It's nothing spectacular if you don't have the right company," Wyatt commented after seeing her face. "Let me hold Scarlett. The trail is over here."

"I'll keep that in mind," Aubree replied.

"It's the inside of the cave that's cool—not the outside." He kicked at a dying bunch of grass and winked at her.

"Am I that easy to read?" Aubree frowned and followed Wyatt to the entrance of the cave.

"Nah, I'm just making conversation." He chuckled.

They stopped in front of a wooden sign indicating that the elevation at the Ice Cave was 7,815 feet. Wyatt had told Aubree to bring a jacket and he handed it to her.

"Now's the time to put this on." He adjusted a stocking hat on Scarlett's head. It was one of his, and the blue knit had to be folded nearly in half to keep from going over the baby's eyes. "It's forty degrees inside the cave. It'll feel nice to us, but I think Scarlett will like having her hat and blanket."

Aubree followed them around the face of the rocky hill. The dirt path ended at a wide cave entrance. A jagged lining of large rocks made it appear as if some giant had pulled the stone apart to get into the dim cavern. Pulling her arms through the jacket, Aubree shivered as an icy stillness surrounded them. She tucked the blanket around Scarlett, and the baby giggled when Wyatt blew warm air on her cheek.

Inside the cave, their eyes adjusted to the semi-darkness, and they walked down a rough dirt path and across a wooden plank bridge where, according to Wyatt, the temperature dropped thirty degrees within a few yards.

The dirty water under the bridge had bits of ice floating in it. Huge serrated rocks loomed above them, dripping. A pool of water with a sheen of ice stretched out to their right and lapped against the deep crevices in the rocks.

Rubbing her arms, Aubree shivered and said, "I can't believe how cold it is."

Wyatt nodded. "It's this way year-round. No sunlight ever gets through."

Aubree looked down into the murky water and watched her breath coming out in clouds. Scarlett snuggled against Wyatt's shoulder so that only her blue eyes peeked out beneath the stocking hat. They walked about twenty-five yards until Aubree could see strands of sunlight ahead. The dark cavern opened up, and the blue sky looked down on them. It was as if someone had taken the top off the cave. They were still completely surrounded by rock, but the ceiling of the cave was gone. There was a slight temperature change, but it was still cold—cold enough that an eight-foot drift of ice-encrusted snow stretching twenty feet wide was wedged against the wall of rocks.

"Now, before you get disappointed at the end of our fantastic cave here, I have something to show you." Wyatt pointed at a pile of rock just inside the darkened portion of the cave. "Here's something most people don't know about."

Aubree followed Wyatt back into the semi-darkness and watched as he crouched down and appeared to be looking at the wall of rocks before him.

"Look, Scarlett." Wyatt pulled out a flashlight and clicked on the beam of light, making it dance along the rocks. Scarlett turned her head and laughed, pointing at the bits of light.

"Most people haven't played shadow games with flashlights before?" Aubree placed her cold hand on the back of Wyatt's neck, and he inhaled sharply at her freezing touch.

"No, look down here." He pointed the flashlight at the wall again, but this time it went beyond the rocks. Past the darkness, Aubree stooped down to see a shallow opening only thirty inches high. She peered into the opening, and the beam revealed a path of sharp frozen rocks that opened into a large cavern.

In the dim beam of the flashlight, Wyatt pointed out piles of more snow and ice. A bit of daylight trickled through a fissure to the right of the cavern. "Have you ever been in there?" Aubree asked.

"I have, and believe me, spelunking and short go together." Wyatt stood and put a hand by his head. "Shimmying all six-foot, five-inches of me through that opening took some doing, and it's pretty cold in there too."

"Is there something to see, or do you just like exploring caves?" Aubree nudged a rock with her toe and reached out to take a wriggling Scarlett from his arms.

"A couple years ago, somebody's little dog went down there and didn't want to come back out. It was an older couple, and I happened to be around, so I got to play 'Hero for the Day' and rescue Fido." He grinned, and Aubree couldn't help laughing as she pictured the tall and brawny park ranger climbing into the cavern to rescue a dog. Then she shivered again.

"I guess we'd better move back into the sunlight," she said. "Thanks for being our tour guide."

Wyatt wrapped his arms around her and the baby. "Anytime. Maybe later today I can show you some interesting rocks around the area."

Aubree raised her eyebrows and tickled his side. "Rocks, huh?"

He kissed her forehead and murmured, "Or twigs, or anything, if it means I get to see you again today." Then Wyatt took her hand, and they walked back into the dry heat of late summer.

Aubree smiled wider than she had in a long time and nudged her worries back a little further from the present. Tomorrow she'd get to work hunting down her hunters, but today she was happy to leave those memories frozen in the ice cave.

Shadowed by the light above the flimsy trailer table that night, Aubree read through all of her notes. Being with Wyatt had put her at ease, and being rid of the hunted feeling she'd grown accustomed to seemed to have given her clarity and a new hope to look for answers in her case. She prayed for help to remember every detail of the conversation from Devin's cell phone. As she meditated, her mind cleared, and she was back in her car listening to the voice responsible for the murder of her husband and the secretary of defense.

Aubree pieced together the fragments from her memory and tried to write out the whole conversation yet again, from beginning to end. Then she highlighted words that might be useful to search on the Internet. She also tried replacing some of the words with synonyms to look for double meanings within the context of each sentence. If there was some type of code hidden in this fragment of conversation, she was determined to find it.

After picking her brain for every detail and trying several different methods, the FBI specialists had never been able to help her remember the entire phone call clearly. Aubree massaged her temples and tried to sort out her thoughts. Maybe it didn't matter what the man had said, but how he'd said it. She still felt suspicious about Governor Ferrin because his voice sounded so similar to the one from her memory. She planned to check him out on the Internet tomorrow.

With phrases from the conversation running through her head, sleep was hard to come by, but Aubree kept repeating, *Tomorrow, I'll find out what this all means.*

TWENTY-TWO

* * *

THE RIDE OUT OF the Paris Springs campground the next morning had Aubree on edge. She looked out the window and then
behind them. It was the closest she'd been to civilization for nearly
three weeks.

"You can relax," Wyatt said. "I didn't see any suspicious characters
this morning."

She knew he was joking, but the nervous jitters threatened the contents of her stomach. "I'm afraid I'll find something, and then I'm afraid
I won't."

"Have you thought about contacting the FBI?"

"Not yet. I doubt they've found anything new since I left, and Jason
would just want me back in protective custody."

Wyatt chewed on his bottom lip. "If you feel up to it, I'd really like to
drive you into Logan next week . . . maybe to meet my parents."

"Are you asking me on a date?" Aubree pinched his side and
laughed.

"Hey! Yes, a date. That's a great idea." He looked to the back seat
where Scarlett's car seat was buckled. She was sucking on the pink ear of
a stuffed rabbit. "Scarlett, how would you like to go on your first date?"

Aubree smiled. "She'll need a chaperone."

"I was hoping you'd say that."

At a café in Garden City, not far from the shores of Bear Lake,
Wyatt ordered some French fries and played with Scarlett. Aubree
settled in a corner where she could see them. The first thing she did

when she sat in front of the computer was type in a name: Governor Brent Ferrin.

Aubree found what she was looking for much faster than anticipated. The information about the governor's immediate family read typically enough until she scrolled down to his siblings. Aubree gasped when she read about the governor's family.

She focused on the seemingly insignificant piece of information—his brother was chief of police in San Diego. She read about how the Ferrin family enjoyed serving their country in many ways. It was much more than coincidence. Aubree knew even without hearing his voice that she had stumbled onto something dangerous.

Thinking back to the assassination of Robert Walden, Aubree remembered seeing many units from the San Diego police department on hand for crowd control. She tapped the keyboard with her pencil and wrote a few ideas in her notebook. Her pulse quickened with excitement as she wrote her assumptions. The chief of police would definitely be involved in smoothing the way for a visit from the secretary of defense to his city. But Aubree wondered if Chief Ferrin had been preparing in a different way.

Then she shook her head. What reason would the chief of police have to orchestrate an assassination of the secretary of defense? Aubree surmised that the FBI would have checked out Governor Ferrin's siblings, and they might even be keeping an eye on the chief of police, but Aubree figured he would be more than helpful and have a pristine record.

She felt pretty sure the San Diego chief of police would be one of the last people the FBI would seriously investigate for this crime—or maybe not. Either way, everything pointed to someone infiltrating the system. The witness protection program hadn't stopped him; the police and FBI hadn't stopped him—maybe because he was working right along with them.

But why? Why was she such a danger? Not just because of his voice. There had to be another reason. Aubree massaged her forehead in her hands and glanced at the notes scribbled all over her notebook. There was something more. She had already decided that, so she couldn't get hung up on Chief Ferrin. The pages of her notebook rattled as she flipped through them. She paused on the transcript of the original conversation from Devin's cell phone.

"What if there's something I'm missing in this conversation?" she mumbled to herself. She looked up to see Wyatt grinning at her with raised eyebrows. She shrugged, and he saluted her and turned back to the window to keep watch.

It was a long shot, but Aubree decided to perform a keyword search on the Internet. The FBI had used several decoding programs to do the same thing, but Aubree wondered if there was something she had missed that would have affected their search. She could enter some of the words from the conversation to see if it helped trigger her memory in case she had missed a meaning somewhere.

She separated each word and typed it in capital letters into Google's search engine. It was tedious at first, but she was determined. She scanned through page after page of search results, not really knowing what she was looking for. Nearing the middle of the handwritten conversation, Aubree leaned her head in her hands. Was she just wasting her time? She thought about skipping the next line. It didn't seem important that the man had said, *"By the time they find him, we'll be in the green."* But then she looked at the sentence again.

It was odd, but she didn't remember placing any significance on the word "green," and now it seemed to be jumping from the page as if it didn't belong.

"In the green" meant money, didn't it? That's what Aubree reported hearing—something about money—but he hadn't said the word money. *In the green.* Could something so simple be the reason for this madness? Her finger rested on the phrase she had written in the battered notebook. Why had she never examined that part of the conversation before?

Aubree entered the phrase "in the green" and scanned through the hits the search engine brought up. Then she decided to focus on just one word, *green*, and she combined it with *conspiracy theories.* She opened another page for a Google search and typed in "green government programs." Her hands shook as she clicked back and forth between the two searches, scrolling through the first page of results.

The search for "green conspiracy theories" didn't bring up anything interesting—instead it concentrated on why people weren't going green to save the earth. Clicking back over to the search for green government programs, she saw several pages with titles such as:

A green government, environmental programs, and legislation. She scrolled through pages of Google searches trying to find something that made sense.

Deciding to modify the search a bit, she switched the words around and typed "government programs green" in the search bar.

The search was redirected, and a new page popped up. At the top, underneath the colorful Google logo, Aubree read, "Did you mean: Government programs GREANE?"

GREANE was hyperlinked, and so she clicked on the strange spelling of the word to see where it would lead. The next page caused her throat to constrict, and the tension made it hard to breathe. She scrolled down the list, and let the mouse hover over the link to a blog. One click displayed www.rachellewrites.blogspot.com with an entry titled, "The New Governor of Nebraska is in the GREANE."

Aubree scanned the contents of the blog, reading faster and faster as her mind tried to process the words. She felt the hairs on the back of her neck stand up. She clicked on a few other areas within the search and read all about the new GREANE deal. There were also several reports bad-mouthing the new governor of Nebraska and his single-minded campaign to be part of the GREANE program.

Aubree looked at her battered notebook again. Her thumb brushed against a smudge of dirt beside her writing and she concentrated on delving into her worst memory. The day Devin was killed had been a terrible day. The FBI had questioned her over and over during the course of the following months, trying to help her remember every single word in the conversation she had heard. She had pieced together fragments of the memory and tried to tell them word for word the entire chilling conversation—at least she thought she had.

Looking at her notebook, Aubree realized her mistake. In the transcription process, she hadn't reported hearing one word because it didn't add any meaning to the gist of the sentence. In fact, she had actually replaced it with the word that fit the meaning she had understood. When she gave the initial report, she had been traumatized. But now, almost a year later, the conversation had come back to her crystal-clear, and she remembered every *single* word.

She realized why the voice had been so easy to recognize when she heard Governor Ferrin speaking on the TV back in Omaha. He'd used the one word she hadn't remembered, and that word had triggered a memory. Flipping back through her notes, she found what she had written about the day she heard Governor Ferrin speak. He talked about a new program, a green program to bolster the state's economy. He said, "The state of Nebraska has a green future." But now Aubree realized that he'd meant a GREANE future.

She looked around the café, and the room seemed to close in on her. Wyatt waved a French fry at Scarlett. Another couple ate their lunch and talked about boating later. She tried to steady her shaking hands as she jotted down notes. She didn't dare speak aloud the one word that she now understood was the reason Devin had been killed. An acronym—*g, r, e, a, n, e.*

After clearing the Internet browsing history on the computer, Aubree picked up her notebook. She walked over, picked up Scarlett, and kissed her cheek. She put a trembling hand on Wyatt's arm. "I'm ready."

He grasped her hand and gave her a concerned look. "Okay. We'll talk in the truck."

They hurried outside, and Aubree buckled Scarlett into her car seat. "I've been looking at this all wrong the whole time." She locked the door and looked over her shoulder again as Wyatt pulled onto the road.

"Aubree, there's no way someone could know where you are right now. Relax."

"But I can't! I just found out the reason my life is in so much danger. It's because of one word—one word, Wyatt!" Aubree pushed her fingers through her hair. "Someone is trying to kill me, not because I heard a voice and could maybe recognize it, but because I heard a word that would identify him."

"What's the word?"

"It's an acronym, and the FBI doesn't even know about it."

"Are you sure? Maybe they've solved the case by now," Wyatt said.

"They never heard the word because I messed up. I thought I remembered what the killer said. *"By the time they find him, we'll be in the money. The intruder will clear the way,"* is what I reported."

"Well, that shouldn't matter—"

"But it does, because he never said 'money.' " Aubree glanced at Wyatt and shook her head. "He said 'GREANE.' "

"Green, like the color?" Wyatt asked.

"No, it's an acronym. GREANE stands for Government Regulated Ethanol: Agriculture for New Energy. It's a new program being developed to create fuel with a higher percentage of ethanol that will be used for a military grade fuel." Aubree pushed the hair back behind her ears and kept talking. "Those areas allowed to participate in the GREANE program will be able to build new ethanol plants to support the demand and bolster the economy of their state.

"The entire administration was for it, but the secretary of defense was talking about putting a cap on the number of ethanol plants built. He was pushing for only one state at a time to run a pilot of the new program to see if it would work."

Wyatt glanced at her with raised eyebrows. "And so you think someone killed the secretary of defense because of this program?"

"I don't know, but I do know that it's more than coincidence that I first heard GREANE from someone who sounded a lot like Governor Ferrin and that his state was awarded a GREANE deal shortly after Robert Walden was assassinated."

She tapped her finger on the dashboard. "I found something on the GREANE program and then I found a post from a blog. It was some blogger spouting off about our corrupt government, and the post wasn't recent.

"At the time, the article said the engineers were continuing to run tests in order to persuade the secretary of defense to reconsider his decision." She glanced at Wyatt, who listened closely as he drove. "I tried to search more on the subject and only came up with a few fragments here and there. The recurring fragment was that Governor Ferrin allegedly bribed someone to award Nebraska the pilot program GREANE. That decision was probably worth a chunk of change to the state of Nebraska and its governor, don't you think?"

Wyatt breathed out a low whistle. "Now you're starting to make me nervous." His face twitched, and he furrowed his brow. "People will do anything for money. But do you really think the governor of Nebraska had something to do with it?"

"From what I could find on him—at least from those who aren't members of his fan club—he's newly elected because he owns some of the ethanol plants in Nebraska and had plenty of campaign money to spare. He wanted to be governor so he could push forward with ethanol production using the excuse that the tax revenue was good for the state, which it was, but he was also lining his pockets. He needed the GREANE deal to pass to further his business. He's the governor, but first he's the owner of several ethanol plants.

"I'm just not sure if the San Diego chief of police is really involved," Aubree murmured.

"The chief? Who's he?"

The breeze blowing through Wyatt's window ruffled the hair near his forehead, and Aubree could smell the scent of pine and charcoal briquettes as they passed an RV camping site. She inhaled and then shook off the fear of speaking the name that might be connected to her case.

"Jared Ferrin. His brother is the governor of Nebraska, and I'm willing to bet my life they sound very alike on the phone." Aubree watched the road in her side view mirror. "I never dreamed of how this would end, but I think I have an idea now."

"What do you mean?" Wyatt gripped the steering wheel. "We can call someone and get this over with. They can get their guy."

"It won't be that easy, or it would've been done already," Aubree said. "If the chief of police is really involved, I'm sure he's covered everything well." She bit the end of her fingernail. "I'm not going to wait for the FBI to figure this out. I think it's time for Scarlett to visit her Grandma."

"But I thought you said they knew where your mom lives," Wyatt said.

Aubree glanced back at Scarlett snug in her car seat. "They do, but my mom is going to take a much-needed vacation."

"I don't think I like where this idea is headed."

"Don't worry. You'll help me think it through." Aubree reached over and squeezed his arm. "It's time for me to stop running."

Wyatt was extra cautious when they picked up their supplies at the grocery store and hurried up and down the aisles. He kept glancing over his shoulder. Once Aubree poked him, and he jumped.

"Just who do you think you're going to see?" Aubree teased. "A guy with a ski mask and a gun?"

Wyatt frowned. "I think I'm starting to understand how you feel, and I don't like it. Let's hurry."

"Well, we should be pretty safe," Aubree said. "No one knows we're here . . . yet. But let's talk about this later. How about after dinner?"

"Hmm. What's for dinner?"

Aubree held up a box of macaroni and cheese and a package of hot dogs. "My specialty."

"Then I'll bring my specialty." Wyatt picked up a can of green beans and chuckled.

After the groceries were tucked away in the trailer and they had consumed their gourmet meal, Aubree tucked Scarlett into bed. Then she pulled out a mixing bowl and a whisk. She ripped the tab off a box, and Wyatt looked up. "What are you doing?"

"Making brownies," Aubree said. "I love brownies, and I never make them."

"How come you never make them, then?"

"Because I would eat them."

"What's the downside?"

"The downside could become the upside." Aubree pulled at the waistband of her jeans and giggled. Wyatt rolled his eyes and reached his arm around her waist.

"Fat chance of that happening. You're beautiful."

Aubree laughed so hard that she slumped back into the ugly vinyl seats around the kitchen table.

"What?" Wyatt held up his hands.

"Shh." Aubree pointed to Scarlett and then covered her mouth as another giggle burst forth. "Fat chance." She wiped a tear from her eye and kept laughing. Wyatt slumped down beside her and muffled his laugh.

"It is a fat chance. Now let's get these brownies in the oven." Wyatt tried to help her mix up the brownies, but they both ended up doing more laughing than stirring. Finally, when the dessert was baking, Aubree sat next to Wyatt. "It feels good to laugh. It's been too long."

Wyatt put his arm around her and pulled her close. "It feels good to kiss too. Let's give it a go." He kissed her, but Aubree giggled.

"I'm sorry. Here, let me try again." Looking into his eyes, she leaned closer and blew softly in his ear. Wyatt squirmed and then grabbed her and tickled her until she shrieked.

"Shh, you're going to wake up Scarlett. Let me cover your mouth."

He kissed her until she stopped laughing and relaxed against him. He breathed softly on her neck and left a line of kisses reaching up to her forehead and then back down to her mouth. Aubree ran her fingers through his hair and kissed him until the smell of brownies brought a smile to her lips. "What are the chances we'll eat that whole pan of brownies tonight?"

She felt his mouth smile against hers, and he mumbled, "I think the chances are pretty good—er—fat, I guess."

A few minutes later, Aubree told Wyatt her plan over a pint of Ben and Jerry's vanilla bean ice cream and hot fudge brownies. "I need to report what I've found about GREANE to the FBI, but I'm still afraid there's a leak somewhere, and I can't trust anyone. When I reported recognizing Governor Ferrin's voice, I only talked to Jason via his cell phone, and they found me within a week."

"Do you trust Jason?"

"I've been asking myself the same question." Aubree hesitated. "I think so." She drummed her fingers on the table. "I have to trust him—there's no one else, and it doesn't make sense not to."

"Is there another way you can communicate with Jason?" Wyatt asked. "Maybe you could make sure his supervisor gets the message too."

Aubree cupped her chin in her hand. "That's a good idea, but I can't take any chances with Scarlett. I want her to be with my mom in case something happens."

"Are you still talking about making a phone call or something else now?" Wyatt put his arm around her. "I don't think you should take any chances with yourself either."

"But that's what I'm doing right now," Aubree said. "I don't even know what's going on with my case because I'm on the run." She put her head in her hands and thought for a second. "Help me figure out how to get Scarlett to my mom without alerting whoever is watching her house. I have to make contact with Jason."

She shook her head when Wyatt tried to interrupt. "I'll be using myself as bait, but the people who are hunting me down will only be able to find me through Jason and never in a remote campground like Paris Springs."

"You can't use yourself as bait unless you're going to be making the calls from the police station in Logan—Wait, I have an idea." Wyatt snapped his fingers. "Do you trust me?"

His hazel eyes sparkled, and Aubree looked directly into them and nodded.

"Good, I know how we can keep Scarlett and your mom safe." He looked over his shoulder at the sleeping bundle on the bed. "We can take her to Logan to stay with my parents and have your mom come after you've made the call to the FBI."

"But how can we be sure that's safe? I don't want to put your family in danger too." Aubree stood and put their dishes in the sink. Then she paced the small space in front of the table. Wyatt reached out and grabbed her hand.

"You know it's the best chance we have. If you're certain there's a leak connected with your agent, then maybe after you make the call, they'll back off your mom." Wyatt squeezed her hand. "She wouldn't even have to come right away. My parents could take care of Scarlett until you think it's safe."

Aubree leaned into Wyatt and blinked back tears. "I'm scared. This is too big. What if it doesn't work?"

"It'll work. We'll take Scarlett to my parents' house. Then we'll come back to Bear Lake and make the call. We can arrange to meet Jason at Bear Lake, and we'll be safe here in the meantime."

She took a deep breath. "I don't know if it'll work, but I feel like this is my only chance." She spread her fingers on the tabletop. "If I can sound convincing enough, like I have solid evidence of my attackers—maybe it'll flush them out."

"I don't think it will be difficult to sound convincing." He leaned over and kissed her temple. "I can't believe how you figured out GREANE."

"It's like it was waiting there for me. My freedom is encapsulated in those letters and what they stand for." Aubree closed her eyes and tried to imagine how it would feel to be free again—to live in peace instead of having her heart hammer constantly like a hunted animal. She breathed in and out slowly and opened her eyes.

Wyatt watched her and pulled her close. He kissed her softly and murmured, "I love you, Aubree."

She kissed him back, but she couldn't say those words yet. They were lodged in her throat, stuck up against the memory of the life she'd left behind a year ago, and buried in the circumstances that haunted her. Her mind swirled with the thoughts that it was her fault Devin had died and that she was on the run with a baby who would never know her father. She didn't want to think about it, but it came unbidden to her mind. It wasn't fair, but it had happened anyway. She pulled back and looked at Wyatt. "Can we go to Logan tomorrow?"

TWENTY-THREE

* * *

THE FBI HAD ALLOTTED as much man power as they could spare for a solid three weeks, and they still hadn't found Aubree. The possible routes, as well as the number of gas stations and campgrounds, made the task equal to searching for a needle in a haystack. Given enough time, they'd find her, but Jason was having a difficult time convincing Agent Napierski of that. He explained the information they had on Aubree again and expressed how close they were to finding her as he sat in Napierski's office.

"I can't give you any more men, Edwards."

"But it may be too late if you don't," Jason said.

Napierski frowned. "Maybe it already is. Concentrate your efforts on the latest activity we've seen. We can solve this case without Aubree Stewart."

"Yes, sir." Jason walked down the hall and slammed the door to his own office, throwing Aubree's file onto the stack of papers on his desk. They had their finger on a number of connections, but without Aubree, the connections would short-circuit. He needed her to flush out whoever was so desperate to cover their tracks.

* * *

The chill of the morning air was refreshing, but Aubree's mind was occupied imagining every possible scenario of the plan, making it impossible to enjoy the drum of the woodpecker or the rush of the creek outside the trailer. Her insides churned as she packed a small bag for Scarlett.

Soft, brown ringlets poked out of a pile of blankets where Scarlett still snuggled in bed. Aubree finished packing and eased onto the bed next to her baby, caressing her cheek. Scarlett had been the only constant of the past year, and Aubree felt grateful to notice the peace that always surrounded her. Her baby girl seemed unaffected so far by the turmoil of events, and Aubree wanted to keep it that way. It would be difficult enough to meet Wyatt's family, but the thought of leaving her daughter there made her head spin.

The crunch of gravel announced her early morning visitor, and Aubree hurried to open the trailer door before Wyatt could knock. She stepped out with a finger to her lips.

"Oh, you want a kiss?" Wyatt pulled her close and kissed her.

"That wasn't what I meant, but good morning to you too." She relaxed her head onto his shoulder.

"Scarlett's still sleeping, then?"

"She'll probably wake up any minute."

Wyatt rubbed Aubree's arms and smiled at her. "I wanted to come by early because I figured you'd be over here worrying about today."

"You're right." Aubree stepped back and sighed. "Do you think we're doing the right thing?"

"I do. As soon as you're ready, I have a couple more campgrounds to check on the way out. I thought we could grab some breakfast in Bear Lake—my treat." He squeezed her hand and pulled her close to him again. "We can wait to make the call to the Feds until after we've dropped Scarlett off, okay?"

"Okay. Let me change Scarlett's diaper, and then we'll be ready." Aubree pulled him into the trailer after her. "Do you want some orange juice while you're waiting?" Wyatt nodded, and she pulled the quart of orange juice out of the miniature fridge crammed with food from shopping the day before. Scarlett yawned and turned over on the bed. She smiled when she saw Wyatt and Aubree standing there.

"Good morning, sunshine," Aubree said and then swallowed a lump in her throat. She pulled Scarlett into a cuddle and blinked several times.

"You okay?" Wyatt asked.

"Yeah, I was thinking how I've never been apart from her, ever."

"You're an incredible mom, Aubree, but guess what?" Wyatt winked at her. "My mom is, too, and I know Scarlett will love her."

Aubree swallowed again and gave Wyatt a weak smile. "I hope so."

"Ma, ma, ma, ma, ma," Scarlett said and then giggled when Aubree kissed her cheeks.

It was barely eight o'clock by the time they left camp, and Aubree tried to appreciate the quiet of the morning and redirect her thoughts, but her hands clenched with anxiety.

Scarlett acted excited about going somewhere again, and Aubree mentally counted the days they had been at the Paris Springs campground. It had been twenty-two days, and there were only a few weeks left until September. Her time at the campground had to be up soon anyway because the weather wouldn't allow her to stay much longer. It seemed so long since she'd left Nebraska, but it was barely a month.

The crystal waters of Bear Lake came into view, and Aubree noticed a few sailboats out for an early morning turn on the lake. When Wyatt stopped to check on the campgrounds, Aubree tried to keep herself from thinking how nice it would be to stay in one place without looking over her shoulder. It was impossible not to hope, though.

The information she pieced together about Chief Ferrin and his brother, Governor Ferrin, had to be on the mark. It was the only thing that could explain why the FBI had failed to solve the murders. Then again, maybe they did have more information than the last time she'd been in touch with them, but it wasn't likely.

Wyatt was quiet on the drive into Bear Lake, and she knew he was brooding over the same things. She wanted to have so much more time with him. She pursed her lips and shook her head. She wouldn't let Wyatt live this kind of life. If the FBI couldn't find enough to convict the Ferrin brothers, she would have to go on the run again.

Aubree swallowed the familiar jagged lump of tears in her throat and stared out the window. *Please, I want a normal life. Nothing fancy, just something safe with no more running.* She let that prayer echo over and over in her mind as they drove closer to their destination.

An hour later, filled to the brim with raspberry-stuffed French toast, they drove carefully through Logan Canyon. "We're lucky they're not doing construction this summer. They've been widening all these roads for years now," Wyatt said.

"It's beautiful," Aubree responded.

"I promise you don't have to be nervous." Wyatt reached over and squeezed her hand.

"I keep trying to tell myself the same thing." Aubree covered his hand with hers and looked out the window. "So, what did you tell your parents?"

"I told them I met the most amazing, beautiful woman who has a daughter, and that they happen to be members of a witness protection program gone bad and that you needed help."

"And they didn't totally freak out?"

"Well, I didn't say it quite so succinctly to my mom. She was pretty worried, but of course, they said they'd do anything to help." Wyatt leaned forward and rested his arms on the steering wheel. "My mom really wanted to have time to visit with you, but I explained to her about the dangers and how we didn't want a bunch of neighbors seeing you and me and then asking about Scarlett."

"Thanks, Wyatt. I'd like to visit with your parents too. Maybe this will be over sooner than we think."

"Why don't you close your eyes and relax?" He glanced at Scarlett dozing in the back seat. "Follow her example. This is going to be a busy day for you."

Aubree grinned. "We planned this right for her morning nap. She should be happy when we get there." She yawned and then chuckled when Wyatt lifted his eyebrows. "Okay, I'll rest for a minute, but aren't you tired?"

"I'll be fine. I'm used to this by now. Sweet dreams," Wyatt said.

Closing her eyes felt good, and Aubree concentrated on relaxing and letting go of her worries. Her mind drifted to flashes of memories—giving birth to Scarlett, saying good-bye to her mom, moving to Nebraska, buying the old truck and trailer and heading to Idaho, meeting a park ranger named Wyatt Erickson, and allowing herself to fall in love again. She dozed until she felt the gentle vibrations of the pickup stop. She stretched and looked around. "Are we here?"

"Yep, my parents live on the island—which won't make sense to you, but think of it as a sunken island. Every other part of town goes up from here." He motioned to the foothills and mountains rising around them. The streets were lined with shade trees bursting in greenery that would soon turn to autumn shades. Wyatt opened the door for her, and she stepped out. "This is a nice neighborhood. It's quiet."

"I like it. It's not as quiet as the Paris Springs Campground, but it's where I grew up, with the mountains right in my backyard."

"I think I can see why you chose the occupation you did."

Wyatt reached into the backseat of his cab and unhooked Scarlett's car seat. Blue eyes popped open, and a two-toothed grin made him chuckle. "Are you ready to meet some new people?" Wyatt stroked her cheek. Scarlett reached out and grabbed his finger, and she babbled something intermixed with gurgles and a smile directed at Aubree.

He grabbed Aubree's hand and took quick strides to a door on the side of the garage. "I'd take you in the front door, but this draws less attention from the neighbors."

Aubree followed him and tried to calm the jitters in her stomach. They walked through the garage and into the mudroom of the house. She heard a female voice say, "They're here!" and as they entered the kitchen, she saw the smiling face of Wyatt's mother.

She was tall, probably five foot, ten inches, and her hair was dark brown and wavy just like Wyatt's. His dad was the same impressive six-foot, five-inches as Wyatt, with a shiny spot on the top of his head that reminded Aubree of her late father.

"Aubree, I'd like you to meet my parents, James and Felicia Erickson."

"I can't believe what you've been through." Felicia stepped forward and drew Aubree into a hug. "I'm so worried for you."

"Now, Mom, you promised not to be a worrywart," Wyatt said.

"But how can I help it?" She bent over the baby carrier. "How could anyone help it when they look at those blue eyes?" She reached out a finger for Scarlett. "You must be the most beautiful baby in the world, huh, Scarlett?"

"Are you sure you don't want to have the police aware of all this?" James was looking from Scarlett to Aubree with a worried expression.

"Yes, Dad. Aubree knows what she's doing—that's why she's still alive."

James shook his head. "This is like one of those FBI stories I like to read, and they don't always turn out right."

"That's why we're taking this precaution," Aubree said. "Believe me. If I knew of a safer way, I would do it."

James held out a cell phone. "Here's the disposable cell you asked me to pick up. Are you sure they can't trace it?"

"It's not registered to anyone, so we should be safe." Aubree took the cell phone. "You paid cash, right?"

"Yep," James said. "I'm still not sure about this." James looked at Wyatt. "But I trust you, son."

"We'd better get going, Mom and Dad." Wyatt put his arm around Aubree. "The sooner we're on our way, the sooner we can come back for a nice visit."

Aubree felt her throat constrict as Wyatt unbuckled Scarlett and hugged her. "Now give your mommy a big hug," he said and handed her to Aubree.

"You be a good baby, okay?" She whispered and then looked over the top of Scarlett's head to Felicia. Wyatt's mom blinked rapidly, and Aubree thought maybe she understood how hard this was. Aubree gave Felicia a hand-written note. "This is Scarlett's napping schedule and the foods she likes to eat and some other things to keep her comfortable. Were you able to pick up some formula?"

"Yes, I'm sure she'll be fine. We'll take good care of her, and we won't leave the house." Felicia stepped toward her with tentative hands. "Scarlett, I'll show you Wyatt's old room, and you can play with his favorite puppy dog."

Biting her lip, Aubree placed Scarlett into Felicia's arms. Then she leaned in and gave her daughter one last kiss.

"Wyatt, keep her safe and don't be the hero." James's voice sounded hoarse. "Call for help at the first sign of trouble."

"There shouldn't be any trouble," Wyatt said.

"Yeah, just a simple information exchange is what we're hoping for," Aubree added.

Wyatt hugged his mom and dad. "I'll call you as soon as we're in the clear."

"It was nice meeting you, Aubree." James held out his hand. "You're all Wyatt has talked about these past few weeks, and we're looking forward to seeing you again soon."

Aubree shook his hand and glanced at Wyatt, whose cheeks were pink. "It won't be soon enough, but thank you for your help."

Wyatt's mom hugged her good-bye, and Scarlett looked confused as Aubree walked away. The baby whimpered and then cried. Her dark eyes were pleading with both Aubree and Wyatt.

"It's okay, sweetie. Mama will be back soon. I love you," Aubree said. Scarlett's lip trembled, and she cried louder, holding her arms out. Wyatt guided Aubree through the door, and she brushed her hand across her eyes as they walked through the garage. Her throat was on fire by the time they reached the pickup, and her eyes stung from trying to hold back the tears.

Before Wyatt started the pickup, he leaned over and pulled her into a hug. "It's gonna be okay. Just think about how it will feel to be free again." He kissed the top of her head and wiped a stray tear from her cheek with his thumb.

She stared into his eyes, and her brows furrowed. "I've been dreaming about it for the past year."

Wyatt kissed her and put the truck into gear, and they began the drive back up Logan canyon. The campus of Utah State University loomed ahead of them, and Aubree was surprised at how close it was to the canyon. Within five minutes, she watched the trees change from oak to quaking aspen to fir as they drove further up the mountains. Her chest hurt, and she realized she'd been holding her breath. She'd been thinking about being apart from Scarlett for the first time and hoping she would hold her again soon.

She turned the cell phone over in her hands and mentally dialed the FBI's main number, which would connect her to Jason. She had decided to call the FBI's secure line in case the number Jason gave her before had been compromised. In a few hours, he would be aware of her general location, and she hoped he would be happy about what she had to tell him.

TWENTY-FOUR

* * *

A T 1:45 P.M., AUBREE took a deep breath and dialed the number to the FBI in Los Angeles. Wyatt had insisted they eat lunch first at the Hometown Drive-In he loved, and now Aubree wondered if that had been a good idea. Her stomach felt unsettled as they sat in the parking lot with the AC cranked up. Her heart hammered against her chest, and she let out a whoosh of air when she was finally connected to Jason.

"Aubree? Is that really you? We've been looking all over for you!" Jason said. "Where are you?"

"I'll tell you in a minute, but I want you to know I'm ready to stop running. I need your help."

"That's good to know, because I need you here," Jason said. "I think we've cracked this case."

Aubree paused. "But how? Did you finally seal up that gaping hole you have in your office?"

"Yes, we fired Miranda. We took her into custody and found out who she was working for. Some guy related to the mafia who was trying to bust through the witness protection program. She had a file with pictures of nearly every person our office has placed in the last year."

"That's crazy," Aubree said.

"We really brought down the house. We've arrested twelve people in the last week related to this operation." Jason paused. "We're really close now."

"That's wonderful!" Aubree said. She reached over and grabbed Wyatt's hand, but then the skin on her arms tingled, and her mouth went dry. "But what about Governor Ferrin?"

"We investigated him; he doesn't have anything to do with your case other than having a voice similar to the one on the phone." Jason sounded exasperated. "We have some other leads we're looking into."

Warning bells were going off in Aubree's head, but she didn't know what to do. She had thought out what she would mention over the phone, and the GREANE program wasn't included in that list. Should she hang up and try talking to someone else? She clenched her jaw and said, "I remembered something from the conversation I heard, and I want to talk to you about it."

"What did you remember?" Jason asked.

"I'm afraid to talk over the phone, but I know that Governor Ferrin and possibly his brother have everything to do with my case."

"But why would you think that? Aubree, they're the good guys—a governor and a chief of police."

Squeezing the phone, she said, "I need you to get to Bear Lake, Idaho."

"Idaho?" Jason sputtered. "I need you in San Diego. We're not sure who else might have photos of you, and until we do, you're not safe."

"I'm not going anywhere until I talk to you in person."

Wyatt mouthed, "What's wrong?" and Aubree shook her head.

"There's no reason for me to travel all the way to Idaho when I'm busy solving your case here," Jason said. "We've wasted a lot of time searching everywhere for you. I know you've got a trailer . . . or at least you did."

"But how did you—"

"We're the FBI, Aubree. I figured out the details on your purchase, but I'm surprised you've survived this long. Is someone helping you? Are you with someone right now?"

The pickup was getting hot despite the AC, and Aubree wiped perspiration from her forehead. "That doesn't matter. I have information now, and because of what happened in Omaha, I'm doing this my way."

Jason cursed, but Aubree kept talking. "I want to know how Tidmore was connected to Miranda. And how did bombing the *Midway* have anything to do with the witness protection program and the mafia?" She knew she had him when he paused, and she heard papers shuffling.

"Aubree, I can't tell you everything about our investigation. I know it looks bad because we have a few loose ends, but what do you expect? The leak from Miranda just fell in our laps the day I talked to you. We haven't had time to sort through everything yet."

She tapped the dashboard, signaling Wyatt to get on the road. "That's exactly what I mean. You may have solved a case dealing with Miranda, but you didn't solve my case."

"But we're closer than you think."

"Please, Jason, I need you available to take a call at Hometown Drive-In tomorrow at noon."

"Noon? Are you joking?"

"No, and I'm risking my life here. What if whoever followed me to Nebraska didn't find me through Miranda? I could've died in Omaha. Please do it for Scarlett."

She heard a sigh, and then Jason murmured, "I'll be at this burger joint you're talking about with my guys tomorrow at noon."

"I promise it will be worth your time. It wasn't the voice that mattered this whole time—it was one word—GREANE." Aubree ended the call. "He's coming." She relayed the information Jason had given her. "Now let's toss this cell phone."

"I'll pull over by the marina," Wyatt said. In the event someone did trace the call, they would get to Bear Lake, but not to the Paris Springs Campground.

Wyatt parked the truck, and they walked closer to a marina with dozens of colorful sailboats. After she tossed the cell phone into the water, Aubree hugged Wyatt. "I'm worried that the FBI still doesn't know Ferrin is connected to my case. It didn't sound like they suspected him at all."

"Do you think they know more than they're telling you?" Wyatt ran a hand through his hair and kicked at a pile of sand. "Or is their case merely overlapping yours?"

"I guess we'll find out tomorrow." Aubree stopped and picked a few of the grassy reeds growing near the edge of the water. "I don't want to go back with them to San Diego. I don't want to ever go back there."

"I'm not going to argue with you about that." Wyatt held her close. Aubree pulled apart the weed and blew on Wyatt's face. He tickled her, and she squealed, but he wouldn't stop until she fell onto the sand and cried for mercy.

They sat on the small sandbank and watched the azure waters of

Bear Lake lap softly against the beach. At first it was quiet, and then Aubree sensed Wyatt wanted to say something. Her nerves had been so tight all day that she felt frazzled and tired. She leaned into him. "What's on your mind?"

"Where do you want to go when this is all over?" he asked in a low voice.

She wanted to say, "Anywhere Wyatt Erickson decides to go," but her heart clamped down on that hope, and she struggled to speak. "I'd like to stay with my mom for a while and sort things out. Give her a chance to see Scarlett and maybe get rid of all the memories haunting me."

"Oh—that's probably a good place to heal." His voice sounded a bit strained, and Aubree wanted to reassure him, to tell him she loved him too, because she hadn't earlier, but she couldn't. Until she knew for sure that her case was closed, she wouldn't do that to him. She changed the subject before the silence became awkward.

"I want to call my mom and let her know I'm okay."

"I think that's a great idea, and we know my phone is safe." Wyatt handed her his cell phone. "Do you want to call from here or on the way back?"

"I'll give her a call from the truck. Let's go."

He stood and pulled her up from the sandy bank. Aubree noticed he hesitated a second before pulling her close to him again, and she felt guilty for hurting him.

"Wyatt," she looked up into his handsome face and noted how the gold flecks in his eyes stood out against the green. "I want to thank you for everything. I hope I'll get a chance to make it up to you soon—you've gone way beyond the duties of any park ranger I've ever heard of."

"It's been my pleasure." He leaned toward her, and she closed her eyes, but then she felt his lips on the top of her head. They walked back to the pickup, with Aubree berating herself the whole way, wishing she could stop being afraid and tell him how she felt. She could see the confusion in his eyes, the disappointment that maybe she thought of him as only a helpful, handsome park ranger who'd given her something to do for the past few weeks.

He opened the door for her, and she smiled. He smiled back, but it didn't quite reach his eyes. Aubree picked at a loose string on her shirt as she dialed her mom's number. There was nothing she could do until this was all over.

"I'm going to tell her I'm safe and to be ready to leave soon," Aubree said as she listened to the phone ring.

"Hello, Mom." Aubree held the phone away from her ear when Madeline Nelson shrieked, "Aubree, you're alive!"

It was difficult to hold back information from her mom and keep the call short, but Aubree promised Madeline she would see her soon. James and Felicia had all Madeline's information if something were to happen to Aubree and had directions to call her if they didn't hear from Wyatt within forty-eight hours.

"Mom, I know you want to see me, but I want to make sure things are safe first. There's a chance you could be followed, and I don't want to take that risk. I'll call you as soon as I can."

"I wish I could leave now," Madeline said. "But you're right—these people found my house before—I'll wait for your call."

"I feel bad making you wait, but I wanted to let you know I'm okay. The cell service is sketchy, so I'd better go. I love you, Mom."

"I love you too, dear, and I won't stop praying until I see you and Scarlett." Madeline hung up the phone, and Aubree hugged herself.

"If this all works out, I may be able to see my mom for the first time in almost a year." She looked at Wyatt. His eyes crinkled in a half-smile, and then he turned his attention back to the road. Aubree stared out her window and wondered what she should do. She put her hand on his arm. "I'm sorry I dragged you into my mess. It's too dangerous. I shouldn't have—"

"Aubree, don't. I'm worried sick about you, and I wouldn't want you doing this by yourself no matter what the circumstances are."

"Thank you." She squeezed his arm and then leaned her head back. It was all too much; her mind was spinning with so many possibilities. She hoped there would be a chance to undo the hurt she'd inflicted on Wyatt in her effort to keep him safe from whoever was after her. Aubree held back the tears threatening to reveal her pain.

He dropped her off at her trailer and said he had to do a few things, but he'd be back in a few hours. Aubree waited until he left, and then she lay on the lumpy mattress and cried herself to sleep.

Scarlett was everywhere in her dreams, and she kept rolling over to cuddle with her and coming up empty-handed. She dreamed her mom was coming to visit at the campground. In the dream, Wyatt helped her prepare a Dutch oven dinner, and they waited anxiously for Madeline to arrive. A light knock on the door sent Aubree's heart into her throat—she was finally going to see her mother. She went to the door and opened it with a smile, but Madeline wasn't there. It was a man wearing a dark hooded sweatshirt and laughing—a horrible gruff cackle. Aubree screamed. In her dream she heard a loud noise and hurried footsteps, and then someone shook her.

"Aubree, wake up. It's Wyatt. I've got you. You're safe."

She struggled to open her eyes, and when she realized it really was Wyatt holding her, she sobbed. She held on to him, and he pulled her into his lap and stroked her hair. "Shh, it's okay."

He rubbed her arms, and she murmured, "It was another dream. He was in it. Wyatt, I'm scared. I hope we did the right thing." She snuggled into his chest and took a deep breath.

"I think we did. I think it's going to turn out right," he said. "I'm sorry; I shouldn't have left you alone. That was a stupid thing to do."

"No, it was my fault." Aubree looked up at him. "I pushed you away because I didn't want you to get hurt if I have to run again."

Wyatt stopped rocking and looked at her.

"I'm sorry, Wyatt, what I should have done—"

"Shh." He put a finger to her lips. "I understand. It's all happened too fast, and I don't want you to be unhappy."

Aubree sat up and put her hands on his cheeks. "It's not too fast. It's been wonderful, like a dream. But with my husband and everything that's happened . . . . I guess that's why I've held back. I keep thinking it's just one of my rare good dreams, and I'm going to wake up and he'll be there laughing again, waiting to kill me."

"I won't let anyone hurt you. You'll get through this, and then you'll be on your way. You and Scarlett can live in a house instead of a camp trailer." He chuckled.

Shaking her head, she smiled. "I should've said this the first chance you gave me. I don't want to be on my way. I love you."

Wyatt's eyes widened, and then his cheeks lifted with a familiar bright smile. He pulled her close and kissed her. His chest rumbled, and Aubree realized he was laughing or crying or both, since he looked happy, but a few tears rolled down his face. She kissed him again and then pulled back to look at him. "I'm sorry I didn't say it sooner."

He shook his head. "Aubree, I love you, and I don't care what happens. I want to be with you and Scarlett. But you're gonna have to make it up to me, because that was a pretty nasty trick to pull on a guy as soft-hearted as I am."

She put her arms around his neck and whispered, "I've been so afraid. Everyone I love is in danger, and I didn't want to drag one more person into the mess."

"We'll get this mess cleaned up, and then you won't have to be afraid anymore." Wyatt kissed her forehead and held her close again. "What time do you want to leave tomorrow to head for Bear Lake?"

"I'd like to get there early, so eleven o'clock should give us plenty of time."

"I'm skipping my rounds tomorrow, except for the ones I can do on the way out. Do you mind if we leave at ten-thirty?" Wyatt said.

"I don't mind at all if you'll come have breakfast with me in the morning." Aubree leaned back and stretched. "I hope I'll be able to sleep after that long nap."

"I could give you a good-night kiss to help you sleep better." He gave her a quick peck on the cheek. "Do you want me to pitch a tent outside?"

"No, I'll be okay." She yawned. "See, all this stress is catching up to me. I'll sleep fine if I can stay away from the nightmares."

Wyatt kissed her again, this time on the mouth, and Aubree tightened her embrace and thought about how much she loved him. A shard of fear still nagged at her heart, but she was through giving into it—it was time to live her life again. She was ready to hope for better things, and Wyatt was one of those. He kissed her until her heart raced faster, and it was the first time in a year her breathlessness wasn't caused by fear.

TWENTY-FIVE

✳ ✳ ✳

NERVOUS JITTERS MADE IT difficult for Aubree and Wyatt to enjoy breakfast the next morning, and even though they tried to talk about other things, it was pointless. Aubree worried about what she would tell Jason when they met, and then she worried if Scarlett was doing okay. Wyatt worried about both of them. She watched the tension lines crease between his eyes as he chewed a pancake drenched in maple syrup.

"Maybe when this is all over, we could have a real dinner date without anxiety for the main course." Aubree lifted up a forkful of pancakes and half-smiled.

He grinned. "I think that's the best thing I've heard all morning. Have you ever eaten at the Bluebird Restaurant in Logan?"

"I doubt it. I don't remember ever going to Logan. We always came to Bear Lake through Idaho."

"Well, then, that's where we'll go. Your mom would love it. I know my parents do." He took another bite of pancakes and a swig of orange juice. "That's how we can keep our minds busy today—let's plan some dates."

"I'd like you to come with me to visit my mom and see where I grew up."

"So now we're talking overnighters, huh?"

Aubree blushed and threw her napkin at Wyatt. "I think the tree house I played in is still semi-sturdy."

"Hey, that sounds like a deal." Wyatt flicked the napkin back at Aubree.

She looked at her watch and frowned. "I miss Scarlett so much. She's probably eating her breakfast and wondering where her mommy is. I hope she's okay."

"Why don't we call on the way?" Wyatt said. "The cell service is unreliable here, but once we're on the main road it shouldn't drop the call."

"In that case, let's get going." Aubree finished off the last bite of her pancakes.

They left the campground by ten o'clock. Wyatt made a quick loop in his truck and checked out all the campsites. As they exited Paris Springs, Aubree looked toward the fork in the road. To the left were the ice caves and to the right was the road leading to the small town of Paris, only twenty minutes from their destination.

Wyatt stopped at the fee area and emptied the payment box. While he re-locked the box, Aubree noticed something about fifty yards up the road. She squinted and could see a car blocking the road with the hood up. The sun glinted off the silver Corolla, and Aubree had to shade her eyes against the glare.

She could see a man working on the car and sighed. It was terrible to think, but she didn't want to get stuck doing car repairs—she wanted to call and check on Scarlett. But the car blocked their exit, and Aubree knew Wyatt would help. She shrugged as he climbed back into the cab. Maybe it would be something simple.

Wyatt put the pickup into gear, and suddenly Aubree remembered something about the brief bit of training she'd received before entering the witness protection program—*Don't accept things for how they appear. Question everything.* And so she did. "Wyatt, I don't think we should go this way. Something's not right."

"What do you mean? It looks like that guy's having some car trouble." Wyatt pointed and stepped on the gas.

"Just turn left, left!" Aubree shouted.

Wyatt jumped when she shouted and cranked the steering wheel to the left. The momentum made Aubree slide next to him, and Wyatt's expression changed from shocked to knowing. "If you want to sit next to me, I don't have a problem with it." He winked, and Aubree rolled her eyes.

"Keep driving. That's not why I wanted you to turn left. Really, something doesn't feel right. Why would a car break down in the road like that—blocking the only way out of here?"

"I don't know. People do strange things all the time. Maybe he wanted to make sure someone would stop to help him."

Aubree glanced back over her shoulder. "Exactly."

"What? You think the FBI somehow traced you here?" Wyatt said. "That's impossible."

Aubree closed her eyes and massaged her temples. "No—I mean, I don't know. I'm sorry; you must think I'm crazy."

He patted her leg and winked. "Just paranoid." He shied away when Aubree playfully slapped his hand. "You know I'm joking. I'm just as worried as you are. Tell you what, why don't we just drive up to the ice caves? I check up there a couple times a week to make sure there isn't any vandalism or other problems."

"Then what should we do if we come back and that car is still there?" Aubree said.

Wyatt rubbed the bit of stubble along his jaw line. "We'll figure something out."

"I guess I'm keyed up because the end is in sight." She put her head in her hands and sighed.

They were halfway to the ice caves when Aubree heard a loud noise, and the pickup jerked to one side.

"What in the world?" Wyatt held tight to the steering wheel and looked behind him. He gasped. Aubree turned to see what the problem was and screamed. The silver Corolla was only twenty yards behind them, and there were two men inside. One of them was pointing something out his window. Wyatt jammed his foot down on the gas pedal, and the truck jumped forward. A shrieking sound and breaking glass sounded right outside. Aubree saw her side mirror explode.

"They have guns!" she screamed, and then she covered her mouth.

"Get down. They blew out one of my tires." Wyatt sank down in his seat. "Get my cell phone and call 911."

Aubree reached over and unclipped his cell phone from his belt. She punched in the numbers and cried, "There's no service!" Another shot fired, and glass from the back window of the pickup flew everywhere. Aubree shook glass from her hair and looked at Wyatt. It seemed like they were going in slow motion, but it had only been a couple seconds since they spotted the car.

"You're bleeding." She pulled a small piece of glass from his forearm, and he winced.

"This isn't gonna work. The truck is pulling too hard." Wyatt reached under his seat and pulled out his holster. He took out his gun and released the safety. "I'm going to stop the truck, and you've got to run."

"No, I can't," Aubree cried.

"Run to the ice cave and hide in the cavern I showed you. Call for help on the way. I know there's some service when you get near the cave—it's higher ground." He pushed the button to roll down his window and gripped his gun.

"I can't—please don't make me leave." Her voice was a strained whisper.

"You have to. I'll try to distract them. Hold on." He jammed his foot on the gas pedal and swerved to the left hard. The truck spun sideways. Aubree could see out Wyatt's window. The silver Corolla approached fast. "Run! Go now! I know another hiding place close by," Wyatt yelled and then pulled the trigger—shots flew from his window. Aubree paused a second to see his second bullet break through the windshield of the car. The Corolla swerved. Aubree held tight to the cell phone and ran.

TWENTY-SIX

* * *

Mrore shots punctuated the mountain stillness as Aubree ran up the dusty road. Her breath came in short gasps. Glancing behind her, she could see Wyatt by the side of the pickup. He crouched behind his tire, and another shot rang out. Forcing her legs to go faster, she pushed the redial button on the cell phone and kept running.

Adrenaline fired through her veins, and she scrambled up the slope toward the face of the rocky cave. The cell phone still didn't have service, but she kept pushing redial anyway. Just before she reached the opening of the cave, the screen showed one bar.

"Please, please be enough," she said and took in another ragged breath. She pushed the send button once more and watched the cell phone's screen flicker. The phone said it was calling, but she couldn't hear any rings. Aubree stood still and lifted the phone above her head, but it didn't seem to change the reception. As she brought it back down to her ear, she heard a voice: "911, is this an emergency?"

"Yes!" Aubree screamed, "Come to the Paris Springs Campground, to the ice caves. They have guns—they're shooting at us."

"Are you injured?"

Aubree took a breath and looked at herself—there was blood on her shirt, but maybe it was from the cut on Wyatt's arm. "I don't know."

"How many people are injured?"

"Wyatt was bleeding from a cut on his arm . . . hello?" Aubree looked at the phone and saw that the call had been dropped. She wondered if the dispatcher had collected enough information to find them.

She hit redial again, but then she heard another gunshot. Her heart felt like it was lodged in her throat, and she looked around wildly. There was no one in sight. Wyatt had told her to hide in the ice cave, but what if he was hurt? She looked around once more and then stepped into the cool darkness of the cave.

Dripping water echoed off the walls, and she stepped wide to miss a large puddle of water. The cave looked much the same as before, but she shivered as her breath hovered in frosty clouds. She stared at the narrow opening to the hidden cavern, and her stomach did a flip-flop.

Crouching down to peer into the depths made her abdomen clench even tighter. It was dark, and Aubree only had the light from Wyatt's cell phone. She hesitated for a minute and tried to decide what to do. Maybe she could climb higher on the mountain and get another call through.

She sat back on her heels and looked at the opening. Her ears pricked up at the sound of approaching footsteps. She scrambled into the opening on her hands and knees, scraping her back on the low-hanging rocks. The frozen ground bit at her palms as she shimmied inside the cavern. Pulling her legs in tight beside her, she stopped to listen. She felt disoriented in the inky blackness of the cavern, and she strained to see the opening she had just slid through. A noise like shattering glass echoed through the chamber, and Aubree knew someone else was in the cave. Whoever it was had stepped on the frozen shards of ice littering the walkway.

She extended her hand above her head to gauge how much room she had to move. There was only a six-inch space before she made contact with another piece of solid stone. Aubree tried to remember what the cavern had looked like when Wyatt pointed his flashlight inside—it was narrow for a few feet, and then it gradually opened up to a small chamber.

Straining to hear any sound, she moved across the rock floor. Every scrape was amplified, and she wondered if she should stay still. There was definitely someone walking through the cave, but if it were Wyatt, he would have called out for her by now. This thought made her pulse race again, and she decided to keep moving away from the opening.

"Aubree Stewart, are you in here? The paramedics are on their way to help your friend. He said you might be in here," a man's voice called through the cave.

Aubree tensed and held her breath. Tears stung her eyes as raw fear overcame her. Now she was certain someone had entered the cave, but she also knew he wasn't here to help her.

"Are you hurt?" the voice called out again.

She didn't fall for his trick for even half a second. Memories from a year ago assaulted her, and she felt dizzy with fear.

"I think your friend is hurt pretty bad. He was calling for you."

Aubree thought about the sound of his voice, mentally comparing it to the voice she heard on TV. Governor Ferrin sounded slightly different, perhaps he spoke with a bit of a Midwestern drawl, and this man's speech was clipped.

The deadpan voice continued, "It's okay to come on out. I was out hiking and saw the action and said I'd help."

Aubree listened to him walking through the cave. He had probably made a full search and was surveying for exits.

"Well, I guess if you're not going to come out. I'll have to find you."

As if she'd been cattle-prodded, Aubree scrambled farther into the cavern away from the menacing voice. She moved stealthily, marking every sound and listening for his movement.

"Aubree Stewart, I saw you come in here. It's dark, but I'll find you eventually." The voice rang through the cave. "You've messed up my plans Mrs. Stewart—oh, I guess its Ms. now isn't it? Sorry about that." He laughed, and Aubree's muscles froze at the sound. She braced herself as he continued speaking.

"Your friend is out of commission, so you may as well come out now. I mean that in the permanent sense—he's taken a leave of absence." The gruff cackle echoed off the walls of the cavern and grated against Aubree's ears.

She clamped a hand over her mouth to keep from crying out. He was lying—he had to be. She wouldn't believe Wyatt was dead—that this horrible monster had murdered another man she loved. She sucked in a breath, realizing he would kill her too.

As if he had heard her thoughts, he continued, "I don't want to kill you, Aubree. I just need to talk to you." His voice seemed to move all over the cave. "That cute little baby of yours is probably missing her mommy, don't you think? Would you like to see her?"

Aubree's teeth pressed into her lip until it stung, and then she took a shallow breath. He didn't know where Scarlett was. There was no way. He was bluffing. She noticed he hadn't said Wyatt's name and must not know it, or he would've used it to coax her out of the cave. If he didn't know Wyatt's name, then he didn't know Scarlett was staying with the Ericksons.

She continued to crawl as he spoke until she reached the far wall of the cavern. A sliver of light came from a crevice above her and she willed her eyes to see through the thick darkness, but she could barely make out a rock a few feet in front of her.

"You're probably wondering how we found you." He chuckled, and his voice sounded a bit closer. "Cell phones—that's how this whole mess got started, and that's how it's gonna end."

She wrapped her arms around her legs and pressed her face to her knees to keep from shivering in the icy darkness of the hidden cavern.

"You must have some kind of a lucky charm, because you weren't supposed to make it this long."

She heard him step around a pile of rocks and a few pebbles scattered down the trail beside the hidden cavern. Holding her breath, she shivered and prayed he wouldn't find her.

His voice rose a notch. "You thought you were pretty smart there using someone else's cell phone to call your mom, but you messed up. We picked up a general location on your cell phone signal when you got in touch with her. It's a device I had embedded in her home. See, the Feds were looking for a human leak, not an electronic one. Smart system, but I guess you know that now."

Aubree flinched and then lifted her head from her knees to listen better. He had stopped moving, and his voice carried through the cavern.

"I thought the FBI had you under their thumb, but you were holding out on them weren't you? How long did it take you to figure out what GREANE meant?"

Biting her knuckle, Aubree curled her shoulders inward, wanting to cover her ears to get away from the voice. It seemed the FBI still had a leak, even though Miranda was gone, but it sounded like he was unsure of how much she had told them.

"My brother got pretty excited when the government came up with GREANE. His ethanol plants were starting to feel the crunch from the economy, and then Uncle Sam came up with a brilliant plan."

His brother. So the man speaking *was* Chief Ferrin. Aubree shook her head. What chance did she have of escaping a police officer? He was still talking, and his voice echoed against the walls of the cave.

"The Corn Belt was chomping at the bit to get in line for grants, and then the secretary of defense came up with his part of the plan. He was good friends with the Ohio state representatives and figured he'd offer GREANE to their state exclusively. Pretty low-down if you ask me, but nobody did, so I decided to help Secretary Walden out. My brother pays well for work-for-hire."

Aubree flipped open the cell phone—still no service. She could see only a few feet around her, and the blue glow from the phone confirmed her fears. She was trapped. He kept talking, and although she wanted to cover her ears, she didn't move.

"Then I made a stupid mistake. I dialed the wrong number and shot off my mouth before I realized what happened. I hurried to clean up my mess, but you just kept making the mess bigger."

Aubree's head spun as she tried to digest all the information he was giving her. Why was he telling her so much? If the FBI knew about GREANE, it wouldn't matter if he killed her. He and his brother would still go to jail. Unless he thought she knew more than she really did. The roar of blood pumping in Aubree's ears did nothing to alleviate the chill settling over her body. She tried to think what to do, but he was talking so much she couldn't concentrate.

He was quiet for a moment, and Aubree heard footsteps on the path again. She hoped he was second-guessing himself and that he would consider looking for her somewhere else. Every sound was augmented, and her body felt as cold as the stone around her.

After a few minutes passed in silence, she began to relax—maybe he really was gone. She thought about what she should do next. How long could she stay in this freezing cavern? At first the adrenaline had kept her body warm as she had struggled to crawl to her hiding place, but now the chill of freezing temperatures was taking its toll. She hugged herself and rubbed her arms to generate some heat.

She was just stretching her legs when she heard footsteps returning. Her heart sank, and she swallowed the tears rising to the surface. She prayed for strength, begging God to spare her life for Scarlett's sake and pleading for Wyatt's safety. She heard a groan and some curse words, and then he started talking again.

"Aubree, come out, come out, wherever you are." He laughed, and the familiar gruff cackle that had haunted Aubree's dreams for the past year echoed through the cavern. Aubree's skin crawled with goose bumps. "This isn't a game. I really need to talk to you. Now where could you be hiding?" Then she saw a beam of light. The hair on the back of her neck stood on end, and her throat constricted as she watched the light from his flashlight trying to break into the darkness.

She had scooted her way into the far corner of the cavern, and the light illuminated a large boulder to her right. She ducked behind the boulder and her shoes scraped against the rocks. The light danced around the rocks. He must have crept along the crevice of the cave and knelt down to look in the opening. Aubree hoped he was too large to fit through the narrow opening. The Internet only showed pictures of his brother, and he was of average height and build.

"If you want something done, apparently you have to do it yourself. So I'm not going to waste a lot of time here. I realize it was my fault. I'm the one who dialed the wrong number, but you should've spoken up sooner. I had it all set up so my brother and I could cash in.

"We just needed someone to get the secretary of defense out of the way. I was going to take an early retirement and head to the Bahamas. But now I guess Europe will have to do. A private investigator can do pretty well over there."

He grunted and cursed again. "I'm surprised you were able to put everything together." His voice bounced off the walls of the cavern, and Aubree couldn't tell how close he was or if he'd tried to crawl through the opening.

"I'm a betting man, and I'm betting that you haven't filled anyone in on that last detail you figured out. You were waiting to do it in person, so the information wouldn't get into the wrong hands, right?

"Well, they might find enough evidence to convict my brother of some bribery scandals, but unless you identify my voice in a line-up, there's not enough evidence against me, and they can't really line up Robert Walden's death with any of the GREANE business you know about."

With a shudder, Aubree realized her hunch was correct—Chief Ferrin thought she knew more about GREANE than she did. She wished she could cry out that she didn't know, but he would never believe her, and it would give away her hiding place. Aubree tried to curl into a tight ball behind the rock.

Chief Ferrin coughed. "You should've known the fall-out would be too big from something like this. Hank would've found you if I hadn't. His best buddy is cold, hard cash. I told him I bet I could find you before the Feds."

Who is Hank? Aubree wondered, but her thoughts were cut short by the sound of a boot scraping against rock. As he was talking, he had shimmied his way into the cavern.

"I'm just lucky I'm willing to bet your life on it, instead of mine." His voice moved closer to her hiding spot.

A deafening shot ricocheted against the cavern, and Aubree covered a scream. Hot tears slid down her icy cheeks as she realized there would be no more running.

TWENTY-SEVEN

* * *

THE ADRENALINE COURSED THROUGH her body now, and she didn't know what to do. He had missed his shot, but she didn't know if he could see her. Aubree didn't dare lift her head to see where he was. She tried to quiet her breathing. Her ears were ringing from the echoes of the gunshot, and she knew Chief Ferrin was moving closer. Her chest hurt from holding her breath, and the tension pounded in her head.

She heard movement a few feet in front of her and shrank against the rock.

"I'm tired of playing hide and seek—found you." His light landed on her foot sticking out from behind the boulder.

Aubree looked up and screamed. When the beam of light moved, she saw the glint of a gun in his hand. He was going to kill her.

"You picked the perfect spot to hide a dead body—better than a manhole." His deadpan voice punctuated the stillness.

Someone grunted, and Aubree heard rocks skitter across the ground. Then she heard Wyatt's voice shout, "Aubree, move!"

The light tilted. Chief Ferrin looked toward Wyatt's voice and pointed his gun. Stifling a scream, Aubree dove to the other side of the boulder as gunshots reverberated through the chamber. She covered her head with her hands. Then she crawled toward Wyatt's voice and the only way out of the cavern.

Someone moaned. Aubree sat still for a minute to get her bearings and listened.

"Aubree, hurry. I don't know if I hit him." Wyatt's voice sounded strained and frantic.

She crawled as fast as she could against the jagged rocks, trying not to cry out as the frozen earth dug at her skin. She didn't know where Chief Ferrin was, and she couldn't hear anything from behind. She headed for the beam from the flashlight on the ground and hurried to pick it up, shining it around to see where Wyatt and Ferrin were.

The light illuminated a body sprawled in front of the boulder she had been hiding behind. Chief Ferrin wasn't moving. She focused the light on his body, but it was too dim to see any blood or gunshot wounds. She turned back to Wyatt.

"I can't tell if he's alive—" She stopped when the light fell on Wyatt's legs covered in blood. "Did he shoot you?" Her voice caught in her throat.

"It looks worse than it is, but I need you to help me get out of here," he whispered. "It's my leg. I don't know where the bullet hit me, but I'm losing a lot of blood."

She felt the color draining from her face but hurried to his side. The low ceiling of the ice cave crowded the small space where he lay just inside the cavern. "What should I do?"

"Get out and then help pull me out where we can see my injury." Wyatt groaned.

Aubree pointed the flashlight at his right leg and gasped. She pulled the boot from his left foot and then peeled off his sock.

"What are you doing?" He winced and groaned with pain.

"I've got to stop the bleeding before I move you," Aubree explained through chattering teeth. She wasn't sure if the cold or the shock was making her shake, but the skin on her hands hurt as the freezing air touched it.

"Wrap it around the wound. If it's not gushing, it'll slow the bleeding," Wyatt's words were laced with pain.

She made a makeshift bandage with Wyatt's sock, tying it around his leg, and then climbed over him toward the opening of the cavern. She tossed the flashlight out in front of her and then reached back for Wyatt's arm.

"Try to push yourself forward with your other arm." The opening to the cave was too shallow to stand, so Aubree propped herself up on her elbow and pulled. Wyatt's muscular build only moved a few inches, and Aubree groaned. "I'm not strong enough."

"Use both hands," Wyatt said. "I'll push myself with my good leg." He grunted and reached for her. She scooted closer to the opening and pulled as Wyatt pushed against the rocks. They moved a few more inches, and Aubree's head stuck out of the jagged opening. Wyatt breathed heavily. "Now get out and reach back in. You'll be able to pull me out from a standing position."

She scooted across the floor of the cave, gasping every time her arms touched the sharp rocks. Then she positioned her feet on solid ground and pulled, using all the strength she had. He only moved a few more inches and cried out.

"I'm sorry, Wyatt. I'm just not strong enough."

"Try grabbing me under the armpits and count to three," Wyatt gasped. "I'll push as you pull."

She grabbed his torso, counted, and heaved him out of the cavern. She stumbled back and barely caught herself before she tripped into the frozen pool of water.

Wyatt sucked in air and clenched his fists to keep from crying out. She noticed his gun tucked into the waistband of his jeans and reached for it. With shaking hands, she set the gun on the ground beside them and crouched by his leg. Wyatt grabbed her arm.

"I think you should go for help."

"I can't leave you here alone. What about the other guy in the car?"

"There were two others. Chief Ferrin must have come from somewhere else." He closed his eyes and took another ragged breath. "I shot one guy, and I think the other one is still looking for me. I hid in the trees on the side of the road and threw a bunch of rocks around to make noise and then snuck back here.

"I was coming to get you, but then I heard Ferrin talking. I couldn't see where he was at first, and then I figured he'd gone in looking for you."

Aubree scooted closer to Wyatt's leg and lifted the leg of his pants. He winced.

"Don't pull up my pant legs. Get my pocketknife and cut it open by the seam," he said through gritted teeth.

Aubree followed his instructions and inspected his wound. Blood oozed from a gash that revealed muscle fibers. She gagged and looked away.

"I don't know what to do." She tried to calm her trembling voice. "But I got a call out earlier, and someone must be coming. Maybe I can try the cell phone again to see if help is on the way—I don't want to leave you."

His skin looked pale, but he squeezed her hand and whispered, "That's a great idea. But be careful."

"I won't go far." She put a hand on his cheek and hurried out of the cave. The sunlight blinded her for a second, and she shielded her eyes. There was no one in sight. Flipping open the cell phone, she walked to higher ground, willing the bars to increase and give her a strong signal. She took a few steps to the side of the cave but stopped when she heard the sound of tires crunching on gravel and sirens whining.

She rushed back to the front of the ice cave and cried out, "Wyatt, the police are here, and there's an ambulance coming." The first police truck stopped beside Wyatt's pickup and the silver Corolla. The officer stepped out to check the vehicles and Aubree waved her arms and screamed, "Help! We're up here. Wyatt's been shot!"

The police officer jumped back and dashed to his vehicle. Aubree could see an ambulance wasn't far behind the police pickup. She stood on the outcropping of rock outside of the cave for a moment longer as the police approached. A third vehicle, a police cruiser, created clouds of dust as it raced along the dirt road behind the ambulance.

"Wyatt, the police are coming now," she shouted, and then she hurried to meet them. Aubree could feel the adrenaline pumping through the air as police officers spread out in the parking area.

"Bring a stretcher. He's shot in the leg." Aubree shouted at them.

The first police officer approached her with wary eyes. "Is anyone still armed inside?"

"There's a man inside the hidden cavern of the ice cave. He was trying to kill me, and Wyatt shot him. I don't know if he's still alive." Aubree hesitated, trying to think how to explain the situation. These police officers would definitely not take kindly to seeing one of their own shot. "He killed my husband a year ago. He was a dirty cop. He had two other men with him. They shot at us earlier."

The officer bristled. "Miss, I'd like you to go on down to the patrol car and wait." He pulled his radio from the clip on his shoulder and yammered out a bunch of police code Aubree didn't understand. She could see he already thought of her as a possible suspect.

"But Wyatt is in there. I was in the witness protection program, and Chief Ferrin found me and was going to kill me."

The officer stopped speaking and glared at her. "Go down to the patrol car."

Two more policemen ran up the path, followed by a couple EMTs. "We've got a possible armed and dangerous man and a cop down inside." The first officer said and pulled out his gun.

Aubree's lip trembled, and she stepped out of the officer's way as he hurried inside. She looked out at the patrol cars parked next to the ice cave, and her stomach clenched. What if Chief Ferrin could convince these guys that she and Wyatt were at fault?

Another police officer stepped toward her. "Do you know anything about the man in the car down there?" He pointed at the Corolla, and Aubree recognized the slumped form of one of the men who had shot at her and Wyatt earlier.

"Is he dead?" she asked.

The police officer glared at her. "Yes. Do you know how that happened?"

Aubree's eyes narrowed. "He was trying to kill me and my friend, and there's still someone out there with a gun."

"I need you to come with me." The police officer reached for her arm, and she flinched. He paused when more sirens cut through the commotion.

Aubree shaded her eyes against the sun and blinked rapidly, and then she screamed. "It's the FBI!" She knew that the black Hummer rambling up the road toward the cave with sirens blaring, followed by three other unmarked vehicles, had to be federal agents.

The police officer stepped back and pulled out his radio, speaking rapidly. "We've got a possible armed and dangerous man loose near the Paris Springs Campground, requesting back-up."

Aubree ignored him and once again waved her arms toward the convoy of federal agents. When the Hummer screeched to a stop and Jason jumped out, Aubree stepped away from the police officer and slumped onto a nearby rock. Agents rushed past her into the ice cave with guns drawn.

Within minutes, Jason had learned the morning's events from Aubree, and three of the agents were crawling inside the cavern to retrieve Chief Ferrin. Jason crouched beside Aubree. "Are you hurt?"

"Just some scrapes. Jason, they think I'm a suspect." She pointed at the police officer.

Jason stood and glared at the police officer coming out of the cave. "This is a federal investigation. Tell your men not to touch the chief."

"Where's Scarlett?" Jason's eyes widened, and he surveyed the area.

"She's safe. She's not here," Aubree said.

"Are you sure she's safe? Do you need me to check on her?" Jason asked, still looking around as if he might see a baby hiding in the bushes somewhere.

"I'm sure, thank you," Aubree said and then turned her head toward the cave. She wasn't ready to reveal Scarlett's location to anyone. "Please, make sure they don't hurt Wyatt."

"I'll make sure, but I need you to stay right here."

Jason ran back and forth between Aubree and Wyatt. He shouted orders to the local police officers to leave Chief Ferrin alone and find the missing gunman.

Aubree continued to shiver even though the sun beat down on her. After what seemed like an eternity, Jason walked back to where she sat. He was talking on his cell phone. He interrupted his conversation to say, "I want you to come with me. Let's take a look at those scrapes."

"What about Wyatt?"

"The paramedics are taking care of him. They'll bring him out of the cave in a minute." He motioned with his head for her to follow as he continued talking on his cell. Aubree followed him to the Hummer where he looked her over. Other than several surface abrasions from the jagged rocks in the caves, she was fine.

When the EMTs hauled Wyatt out on a backboard, Aubree followed them to the ambulance. Wyatt's skin looked gray, and she averted her gaze from his bandaged leg. "Can I ride with him?" she asked and reached for his hand.

Jason cleared his throat. "I have strict orders not to let you out of my sight." He made eye contact with Wyatt and frowned.

"But—" Aubree protested.

"He might be in surgery for a few hours. You can wait at the hospital with me, and we'll debrief."

They lifted Wyatt into the ambulance, and Aubree scrambled inside. "I just want to say something to him," she told Jason.

She leaned over Wyatt. "I want to come with you, but they won't let me," she whispered.

"They're taking me to the Logan hospital," Wyatt said, and then he grinned at her. "I like your outfit."

Aubree looked down at her shirt covered in blood and dirt. "If you weren't already shot, I'd smack you." She leaned over and kissed him instead.

"Hmm, I think I'm gonna live." He closed his eyes and squeezed her hand.

"I'll see you soon, okay?" She ran her fingers through his hair and touched his cheek. Wyatt nodded, and she could see whatever pain medicine they'd injected him with was beginning to take effect.

She stepped down from the ambulance and followed Jason to the Hummer. As she climbed inside, she noticed several police officers and agents at the mouth of the cave dragging out the body of Chief Ferrin. Aubree cried out and covered her face with her hands.

"I'm sorry you had to see that. I meant to get you out of here sooner. He bled out in the cave from a gunshot wound to the chest." Jason put the Hummer in reverse and backed away from the ice cave.

Aubree's hands shook, and she felt overwhelmed with every emotion that had played out in the ice cave over the last hour. Jason reached behind her seat and handed her a blanket and a water bottle.

"Put this on and take some deep breaths. You're experiencing some shock." He spoke in a low voice and continued to talk to her as they drove away from the campground and out onto the main road. The ambulance carrying Wyatt had left before them, and Aubree concentrated on him and tried to shake off the aftereffects of the adrenaline rush she'd been feeling.

"Did they find the other gunman?" she asked.

Jason chuckled. "Yeah. He was lying in the creek bed with a broken leg. He fell out of a tree. I think he was trying to get a visual from high ground to shoot your park ranger." Jason glanced at Aubree. "It's a good thing Wyatt knew his way around this place, or you might not have been so lucky."

Aubree pursed her lips. "I know."

"Looks like we got here a little late. I'm sorry about everything," Jason said. He kept his eyes on the road as they drove past Bear Lake.

"Actually it was just in time. I was afraid that police officer was going to arrest me. How did you find me anyway?"

"You have so little faith in the FBI, don't you?" Jason smiled, and Aubree rolled her eyes. "Well, we're pretty efficient. But it would've been easier if you had told me." He shook his head. "My office has been trying to hack into the mainframe of Ferrin's tracking system since shortly after you called yesterday. We acted fast, but he disappeared faster.

"When you mentioned Ferrin and then green, not the color, but GREANE, it was like every alarm in the whole building went off. We went straight to Ferrin's home and found a tracking system only used by the FBI—it's new. Somehow he'd gained access to the full system with the tracker in place."

Aubree shivered and pulled the blanket tighter. "I know. He explained all of it to me in the cave to distract me so that he could climb inside the cavern and kill me."

"You're just lucky Wyatt was a good shot. Sometime you'll have to tell me the story of how you ended up with a park ranger." Jason glanced at her and then back at the road.

She blushed and touched her lips, thinking of the last kiss she'd given Wyatt.

Jason paused for a second and cleared his throat. "I guess he'll be taking care of you now?"

Aubree looked at Jason. His jaw was set in a rigid line, and his face was flushed. She felt warmth creep up her neck as she realized that Jason's feelings for her were deeper than she'd understood. She pulled the blanket tighter. How many indicators had she missed that he didn't want to just be her FBI agent? She reached over and touched his hand. "He's a good man. A lot like you. I fell in love with him."

She watched him swallow, and then he nodded. Aubree looked out the window and watched the forest rushing past.

Jason cleared his throat again. "It took all of our techs to discover how Ferrin found you so quickly, and then we knew it would still be heads or tails whether we could get to you first.

"While they were still trying to bust into the mainframe, I headed out and got to Bear Lake last night around midnight. We've been canvassing the area since—praying our techs could break through in time." He reached across the cab and pulled the blanket over her shoulders.

"Of course you had to pick one of the most remote campgrounds around." He shook his head. "You did well."

"I could've stayed there a long time too," Aubree said. "I got a nice trailer."

Jason clicked his tongue and looked at her. "You know we've had our eye on the governor ever since Hank Dennison switched his allegiance from Ohio to Nebraska."

"That's the name. Hank. Chief Ferrin said something about him and I didn't know what he was talking about," Aubree said.

"Hank Dennison is the secretary of agriculture." Jason whistled. "It's what we suspected. Now we'll have the proof we need."

"What do you mean?" Aubree asked.

"Ferrin wanted to kill you because he thought you knew more than you did. Maybe he thought you heard more of the conversation that day on the phone, but he thought you knew that Hank Dennison accepted bribes from Governor Ferrin to award Nebraska the pilot program of GREANE.

"It's what we've been trying to prove for months now, but we could never get the evidence to convict." Jason smiled. "Thanks to Chief Ferrin, we don't need that now. But what I'd like to know is how in the world did you figure out your case was involved with GREANE?" Then he shook his head. "Actually, what made you think green was something other than money in the first place?"

Aubree gave him a sideways glance. "Google and a blogger with some great inside information." She folded her arms and tried to keep her knees from shaking. "I kept writing out the conversation, trying to remember every word. Then when I did a keyword search, I realized the original conversation was "in the green" not "in the money" like I'd reported. I just wish I'd remembered the word sooner. It would've given you the push in the right direction you needed to investigate Ferrin."

"So you do have *some* confidence in us, then," Jason said.

"I guess so." Aubree smiled. "What will happen next?" She asked the question she'd worried about all day.

"We've got to find out who else Ferrin was working with. I guess he wasn't involved with Miranda and her operation at all—other than for buying information. But I think you're safe now. Ferrin was looking for you to protect himself. You aren't a threat to anyone else involved."

Aubree looked at him and swallowed hard. "But what about Dennison? Will I have to testify?" Aubree gripped the armrests with the little strength she had left.

"Not if I have anything to do with it. I think when Ferrin and Hank see the evidence, they'll plea bargain their way out of this and implicate each other in a hurry." Jason checked his rearview mirror. "I want to keep you out of this, and I don't think that'll be too difficult."

"You really think so?"

Jason nodded. "We'll take some precautions while we finish out the investigation, but yes, I think it's time you stopped running."

Leaning her head back against the seat, Aubree felt something inside her break free. The tears escaped from the sides of her eyes, and she didn't wipe them away. Jason said the very words she'd dreamed about for a year. She was ready to stand still and feel safe.

TWENTY-EIGHT

✳ ✳ ✳

"BA, BA," SCARLETT SAID and clapped her hands when Madeline tickled her. Aubree laughed and snuggled in closer to Wyatt on the porch swing of her mother's house. "What do you think of your vacation?" Aubree asked.

"I think my mom's right. I'd better not wait to get shot before I take another one."

Aubree laughed and then looked down at his right leg. It was wrapped tightly in bandages that began just below the hem of his denim shorts and extended to his foot. Luckily he hadn't suffered any permanent damage. It had been six weeks since their run-in with Chief Ferrin.

Wyatt's injury had forced him to take a leave of absence for the rest of the camping season, and then he would have to continue with physical therapy through the winter months. He hoped to be able to return to work by the first of the year.

"It's still hard to believe it's all over," Aubree said.

"Yeah, and that you're responsible for the takedown of a governor, a chief of police, the secretary of agriculture, and a lucrative ethanol business." Wyatt squeezed her hand.

Aubree laughed. "I'm not responsible for any of that."

He lifted his eyebrows. "Well, if you say so."

Leaning her head on his shoulder, Aubree thought about the past few weeks. There had been plenty of questions, but thankfully, because Chief Ferrin had sought her out so ruthlessly, he'd left a trail of information in his wake. He and his brother were involved in some other shady deals but none as beneficial to their wallets as the GREANE program would have been to Ferrin Ethanol production.

Governor Ferrin had been under close watch with GREANE because of the last minute decision to include his state in the pilot program, and now the FBI continued to find new information about the plot and assassination of the secretary of defense. Jason had called Aubree again a few days ago and informed her that ethanol had been just the tip of the iceberg and that this case had agents scrambling all over hunting down new information. Dennison and Ferrin had fulfilled his prediction—scurrying to be the first to implicate the other.

"Once we sort through the lies and cover-ups, we may have something solid to work with," Jason had told her.

"I'm sorry I ran—I should've trusted you," Aubree had said.

"You did all right. They were coming for you from every angle."

"Thanks, Jason, for everything."

"Take care of yourself and hug Scarlett for me."

The FBI had been on the right track all along, but Aubree was the missing link in their investigation. The GREANE program was on hold, but her life wasn't anymore. Aubree smiled as she thought about her life unfolding before her like a clean slate.

"What are you thinking?" Wyatt leaned back and looked into her eyes.

She smiled. "I was thinking about how much I love camping."

"Enough to do it every summer?"

"For the rest of my life," Aubree answered. "I love you." She tilted her face, and he kissed her, creating tingling sensations up and down her arms.

Then he pulled her close and murmured, "I love you, too." She felt his chest rumble with a laugh. "I think I need to plan another vacation. I might call it something else, though."

Aubree lifted her head. "What?"

Wyatt chuckled. "Hmm, I think it's called a honeymoon."

BOOK CLUB QUESTIONS

* * *

1. If you received a phone call like Aubree's, how would you react? How much information would you remember about the caller's voice, dialect, and inflection? Try listening to someone's voice in your head and see what distinguishing characteristic you would use to describe it.

2. As the plot was revealed, did you come up with your own ideas for who was behind it? How close were you to being right? Why did you think one character was more likely to be the criminal than another?

3. In one segment of the book, Aubree tells Wyatt that if she were to die, Scarlett wouldn't remember her. How do you think children are affected when they lose a parent at a young age? How does this possibility influence Aubree's determination to survive?

4. When Aubree meets Wyatt, she struggles with some guilt for having feelings for him after the recent death of her husband. Is this normal? How does she overcome it? Does she make the right choice when she decides to trust Wyatt?

5. Were you surprised when you learned about the multi-layered criminal activity associated with the wrong number? Why or why not? If not, what clues gave it away for you?

6. Do you think Aubree makes the right choice when she ventures out on her own or should she give the FBI another chance to help her? Why or why not?

7. How do you feel about the ending of Aubree's story?

ACKNOWLEDGMENTS

Writing this book was quite the process, and I'm grateful to everyone who helped me reach the finish line.

Patrick and Necia Jolley saw this book in raw form and helped me brainstorm ideas—thanks for your valuable feedback and support. My critique group, Novel Thoughts, helped mold this into a page-turner. Thank you, Cindy Beck, Nichole Giles, and Connie Hall.

I would also like to give a big thank-you to Authors Incognito and LDS Storymakers (www.ldstorymakers.com), who sponsored the first writing conference I ever attended. It's scary to think where I'd be without all the training, advice, and support I gleaned from these two groups.

Thank you to my group of readers, who probably all saw a different version of this manuscript: ToriAnn Perkey, Tina Ellsworth, Jill Clark, Nancy Baird, Heather Justesen, and Tim and Andrea Jolley. Thank you to my editors and all the great people at Cedar Fort for giving me this opportunity.

Finally, I'd like to give a huge thanks to everyone in my family. Mom, Dad, Stephanie, Patrick, and Sarah—I love you. I have the best in-laws—thanks, Nancy and Francis, for your encouragement and love. Thank you, Steve, for listening to me ramble about my writing and being one of my first readers. And thanks to my wonderful children for their patience, for hugging me when I struggled, and for cheering me on every step of the way.

About the Author

* * *

R ACHELLE J. CHRISTENSEN WAS born and raised in a small farming town in Idaho. Her creativity developed easily in this rural area as she spent many years working in the fields with only a few weeds to distract her daydreaming. She graduated cum laude from Utah State University with a bachelor's degree in psychology and a minor in music. Rachelle loves spending time with her family and writing during every spare minute she has. She also enjoys singing and songwriting, playing the piano, running, motivational speaking, and—of course—reading.

You can stop by Rachelle's blog at www.rachellewrites.blogspot.com or visit her website at www.rachellechristensen.com.

0 26575 53641 6